Brian takes some of the gr[...] [...]me and goes beyond just putting words on paper. He interprets and puts his unique spin on each, helping his readers apply the words of the masters to everyday life. Customer Delight 365 will do just that, and do it well. It's 365 of awesomeness that you can find in one place. Thanks Brian for making sense 7 days a week, 52 weeks a year.

~Doug Sandler, bestselling author, Nice Guys Finish First
DougSandler.com

* * *

I've been a buyer in the hospitality industry for over 20 years, so I've experienced a lot of customer service – both good and bad (and occasionally hideous). I wish this book were required reading for every person in a customer-facing role. Brian is absolutely right – when you delight your customers, you create not only loyalty, but ambassadors who recommend you to others. That is the secret to longevity in any hospitality career. Buy this book, and use it for daily customer service inspiration.

~Shawna Suckow, CMP, Top 25 Women Meeting Industry Planner, Speaker,
Author
ShawnaSuckow.com

* * *

This book is a great reminder that it is not our prospects that make us money... it's our customers! Brian Monahan has written the perfect book for daily motivations about how our attitude is the precursor to sales success.

~Sam Wilder, Publisher, Positive Magazine
Positive365.com

* * *

Brian brilliantly recites powerful world leader messages to help readers productively maneuver a winning approach to inspire and enhance the customer experience.

~Deborah Gardner, CMP, Award-Winning Author & Speaker
The Pit Bull in a Skirt!
DeborahGardner.com

Veronica
So Delightful
to meet
you!

CUSTOMER DELIGHT 365

BRIAN MONAHAN

Cover design by Daniel Jones: DanJonesCreative.com

Edited by Ann Weber: RevealingWords.com
Printed on acid-free paper

Brian Monahan

BrianMonahan.net
CustomerDelight365.com
Twitter.com/cdelight365

First Edition

Dedication

Customer Delight 365 is dedicated to my hospitality industry brothers and sisters. The Customer Service profession is not for the faint of heart, but for the delight of heart. May you find your delight and share it.

Table of Contents

Forward

Somebody finally got around to fixing the traditional book of quotations.

If you're an inspiration collector (and I know you are because you're looking at this book), how many different quote books do you own that include a lot of the same phrases? How many times do you need to read the same statement from Abraham Lincoln?

What's missing from every published book of quotes (until *Customer Delight 365*!) is how the quotations personally impact the individual who pulled them together to share with you. Other quote books are missing a unifying voice that shares ideas for putting the wisdom behind the featured quotes into action in your personal life and your business life.

With *Customer Delight 365*, Brian Monahan breathes new life into the old-fashioned book of quotes.

Brian features a few of the old favorites from Ben Franklin, Walt Disney and Albert Einstein, but he also shares the deep wisdom of previously overlooked philosophers like Chumbawumba, Christopher Walken and the wise-beyond-her-years Ella Monahan.

Each page inside *Customer Delight 365* features a daily quote followed by "Brian's Take," where the author adds his own individual insight, experience and context to the timeless wisdom of the quoted individual. Brian explains how the quotes apply to achieving Customer Delight.

This book isn't just a collection of *quotations*; it's a collection of applications and implementations that you can read, examine and put into action.

The only thing missing from the book is your wisdom. Yes, YOU...the reader.

I encourage you to take your copy of the book and use the white space, margins and blank pages to add your own very personal insights on customer service—Customer Delight—to the wisdom within.

All the wisdom in this book of quotes is useless without your intention to make them real. This is a book to not only be read, but also to be lived.

Yes, Brian Monahan finally fixed the book of quotations.

And I'm one customer who is definitely delighted.

Don!

~Don The Idea Guy
www.dontheideaguy.com

Introduction

All jobs contain an element of customer service, but my customer-service career didn't truly begin until I left the Marine Corps. That's when I started working in audiovisual production services in hotels and event facilities.

As my career unfolded, I eventually realized that I wasn't in the audiovisual industry: I was in the hospitality industry. This was a huge distinction that changed my career. With this realization, I transformed my approach to customer service. I no longer was in the business of providing audiovisual equipment. I was in the business of *delighting* my customers. Yes, delighting. To be honest, the insight about delighting my customers came in retrospect. I initially thought of what I was doing as "exceeding the customer's expectations" or "creating customer satisfaction."

As an avid reader of sales and customer-service books, I continually refine and hone my approach to customer service. From Jeffery Gitomer's book *Customer Service is Worthless, Customer Loyalty is Priceless* to *The Spirit to Serve* by J.W. "Bill" Marriott, you'll find volumes of information on the topic. But I didn't stumble on the word "delight" until 2012.

I attended a hospitality conference in 2012, and one of the presenters referenced the book *The Customer Delight Principle* by Timothy Keiningham and Terry Vavra. In their book, Keiningham and Vavra dig deep into the statistics behind customer satisfaction. Customer satisfaction, they say, is way short of the Holy Grail when it comes to creating loyal customers. In fact, if your customers are "merely" satisfied, they might even say you have failed. Why? Just being satisfied is not a factor in creating long-lasting customer retention and growth. They go on to say; however, there *is* a Holy Grail: Customer Delight. Customer Delight not only creates loyal customers, but it also creates customers who want to share your product or services with others.

Upon hearing about the difference between mere satisfaction and delight, a light bulb went off in my heart. Yep, I said *heart*, not head. *Heart* is one of the key distinctions I advocate in this book. In today's over-information age, matters of the heart cut through the clutter. Businesses that learn to harness the power of the heart claim a unique and special advantage. In many ways, this book is a deep dive into a methodology grounded in creating memorable and heartfelt experiences for your clients.

In fact, while writing this book, I tweaked the words to a famous mantra. "Beauty is in the eye of the beholder," we say. Customer Delight, I've determined, is in the *heart* of the beholder. If you grasp this concept, not only will Customer Delight be in the heart of the beholder, but profit will also be in the bank of the "be-giver."

I am so excited to share this book with you. *Customer Delight 365* is going to rock your world! I put a lot of heart and soul into writing this book. It's a lifetime of lessons, successes, failures and inspirations. And it kind of came together by accident.

As of the publication of this book, my daughter is seven years old. I came into my writing voice about the time she was born. This created a mutually exclusive life scenario, in that raising a young child is not really conducive to extended blocks of writing time (much less extended blocks of coherency). After a number of years writing a blog, I determined that my life could only accommodate short bursts of writing.

Fortunately, I "happened" upon a daily devotional called *Jesus Calling*, by Sarah Young. The format is a daily scripture, followed by an inspirational writing. I found it to be very compelling, and it touched my spirit deeply. I discovered a powerful approach to reading the daily devotional when my wife and I started reading the devotional together. It was our daily prayer over dinner, and when we did not share a formal dinner, we kept up with the daily passages individually.

A few months into reading *Jesus Calling*, I started to notice a synchronicity between my wife and me because we were reading the same material, sharing a common thread. Although the daily readings often had a different meaning for each of us, the impact was uniquely different and more effective than simply reading alone.

In a moment of inspiration and desperation, I stumbled onto my idea for this book. My heart was yearning to share my inspirations and life learnings, but after many starts and stops, writing a traditional book was not going to work. I thought to myself, why not create a *Jesus Calling* for customer-service professionals? Not necessarily a religious book, but a book with a definite spiritual element, a "customer-service Bible," so to speak. I saw this book as a tool for members of a group or organization to get in sync with each other through a daily "devotion" (a quote and a passage) on the topic of creating customer delight.

This book is an excellent resource for an individual customer-service professional. I believe, however, that if you leverage the material as a group or organization, it has the ability to change the world.

Because we all learn differently, in the next chapter, I will cover a few methods for reading this book.

But before we move on, I have a question for you.

Are you ready to change the world?

Delightful!

How to Read This Book

There's more than one way to skin a cat, and there's more than one way to learn about delighting your customers. Here are a few methods I mapped out to maximize the impact of Customer Delight 365 for you and your team.

Coast-to-Coast Method:

I know you've been waiting your whole life for this book, and you just can't bear to wait to read tomorrow's daily passage. So I give you permission to dig right in and read the book from cover-to-cover! I applaud your enthusiasm. But once you're finished, don't forget the part about this being a journey. This book will hit you differently on different days of the week. I encourage you to find a way to connect weekly with the book. But by all means, cover-to-cover, coast-to-coast your way through this book.

Daily Dose Method:

This book is set up as a daily devotional, which is the method I am fondest of. I want you to think of this book like a vitamin. A daily dose of delight is a good thing, but 365 vitamins all at once are hard to digest. Yes, I know I already gave you permission to go coast-to-coast with delight, but I am confident a daily dose is the best method for absorbing this content.

The MasterHeart System:

As I mentioned in the introduction, significant power and synchronicity comes from sharing this content with a friend or colleague. You don't need to be perfect; you might miss reading for a day or a week or even a month. Don't fret—it's a journey. Just make sure you come back to the book eventually. The important thing is that you come up with a strategy to share this content with a trusted partner or members of your organization.

One of my favorite concepts from Napoleon Hill, author of *Think and Grow Rich*, is the power of a mastermind. When you bring two or more minds together, a third or additional mind is created, greater and more powerful than the sum of its parts. I like to think of *Customer Delight 365* as a MasterHeart Group: a powerful network of heart-centered customer-service professionals changing the world one customer at a time.

Oratory Method:

Our voices carry a sensory experience that reading alone cannot provide. When we speak, not only do we have an oratory experience, but we can also have a vibrational experience. Because this is a book of the heart, we must experience it differently. When using the MasterHeart Method, try reading the passages aloud. You will notice the act of reading and/or hearing will create a different experience for you and your partners.

Delight Roulette:

Roulette has taken on such a negative connotation with the term "Russian Roulette," but imagine a world with "Delight Roulette."

Open the book and read a passage, or pick a number out of the air and read that page.

The cool thing is, the only chance you're taking when playing Delight Roulette is you might get a paper cut.

Social Delight:

Customer Delight is a team sport, so share your inspirations on social media. Be sure to use the daily hashtag (#CD365Day1…) provided at the bottom of each page. For your convenience, the e-book version of Customer Delight 365 has each day's hashtag is an active tweet. Simply click and tweet!

Be sure to follow me on Twitter @cdelight365 or visit CustomerDelight365.com/social for a complete list of social media options.

January

January 1

"Every artist was first an amateur."

–Ralph Waldo Emerson

Brian's Take:

Day 1 of Customer Delight 365! I'm so excited that you are taking this journey with me. It's my hope that you embrace this journey both as an artist and as a human being.

Creating Customer Delight is akin to an artist in his studio. On a daily basis, we get to paint strokes of color and texture into the experience for our customers. Although I trust many of you who are attracted to my book are already accomplished customer-service experts, I believe the best journey is recognizing daily that we are both experts and amateurs. Today, we begin to change the world!

P.S. I recommend you read this entry more than once a year.

#CD365Day1

January 2

"The market for something to believe in is infinite."

–Hugh MacLeod

Brian's Take:

Hugh MacLeod, a visual and emotional artist, is one of my virtual mentors. His quotes and drawings cut through the clutter and find the essence of business.

This quote has been one of my guiding values since I first read it. This quote speaks to my soul, which is why it's so powerful to me. It not only tells me about the market for something to believe in, but it's also something for me to believe in.

It could also be said, "The market for Customer Delight is infinite."

#CD365Day2

January 3

"Business, more than any other occupation, is a continual dealing with the future; it is a continual calculation, an instinctive exercise in foresight."

–Henry R. Luce

Brian's Take:

Creating Customer Delight is like going back to the future. If you can foresee the future, you're prepared for the moment. Delight grows in the moment, but its seeds are in the future.

#CD365Day3

January 4

"A positive attitude causes a chain reaction of positive thoughts, events and outcomes. It is a catalyst and it sparks extraordinary results."

–Wade Boggs

Brian's Take:

Are you the beginning or the end of the chain? Here's an idea: Consider the chain as a loop rather than having a defined start and finish.

Being part of the loop allows you to be both the catalyst and the receiver of delight.

Don't break the chain! Spark it!

#CD365Day4

January 5

"If you make customers unhappy in the physical world, they might each tell six friends. If you make customers unhappy on the Internet, they can each tell 6,000 friends."

–Jeff Bezos

Brian's Take:

This quote is inaccurate because the two worlds aren't separate anymore. All customers, whether happy or unhappy, have the opportunity to tell 6,000 friends—or the entire world—about their experience with YOU. I capitalized YOU, because YOU have the opportunity to have an unhappy customer or a delighted customer.

What will they say about YOU in the physical and internet worlds?

#CD365Day5

January 6

"Memorable customer service can only take place in a human-to-human situation."

–Jeffrey Gitomer

Brian's Take:

I've had the opportunity to work with Jeffrey Gitomer on a number of projects over the years. But I'll never forget the time he was in Cincinnati for one of his public seminars.

We scheduled an early rehearsal on the day he arrived. Jeffrey knew I was a big fan of his work, and he asked me to join him for the afternoon after the rehearsal. We spent most of the afternoon visiting vintage bookstores, one of Jeffrey's hobbies, and discussing the art of sales. He is a busy man and quite in-demand, so I never thought in a million years he would have even 15 minutes to spare. I will never forget that he took the time to mentor me, personally and professionally. He could have easily brushed me off; instead, he not only created a customer for life, but also a raving fan. A million of his books and seminars will never stack up to a few hours of hanging out. How can you hang out with your customers?

#CD365Day6

January 7

"Always be yourself, express yourself, have faith in yourself, do not go out and look for a successful personality and duplicate it."

–Bruce Lee

Brian's Take:

Authenticity is one of the core principles in Customer Delight. People are intuitive beings by nature. They can sense the incongruence of an inauthentic experience.

In any relationship, we inherently ask ourselves: "Can I trust you?" If your customer senses that you're trying to be someone you're not, they instinctively distrust you. Distrust is an enemy of delight.

Be yourself, your delightful self.

#CD365Day7

January 8

"No act of kindness, however small, is ever wasted."

–Aesop

Brian's Take:

Kindness is the equivalent of a perpetual delight machine.

#CD365Day8

January 9

"Your website isn't the center of your universe. Your Facebook page isn't the center of your universe. Your mobile app isn't the center of your universe. The customer is the center of your universe."

–Bruce Ernst

Brian's Take:

Your marketing is important to you. Your product and service are important to your customers. Don't lose sight of your priorities.

If your website is part of your product or service, remember to include delight. When posting to your Facebook page, ask yourself: "What posts will bring my customers delight?"

Delight is about flipping the focus from you to the customer.

#CD365Day9

January 10

"We all know that successful people come from hardy seeds. But do we know enough about the sunlight?"

–Malcom Gladwell

Brian's Take:

Customer-service professionals generally come from hardy seeds, but these seeds will wither and die without sunlight.

How are you providing sunlight for your precious seeds of delight?

#CD365Day10

January 11

"Without caring, there can be no quality."

¬Joel Barker

Brian's Take:

That's right, a cold shoulder can ruin the best piece of cake. Have you ever eaten at a restaurant with superb food but horrible staff? Once or twice I bet, which, I believe, is where the saying, "Fool me once, shame on you. Fool me twice, shame on me," originated.

Don't be shaming your customers.

#CD365Day11

January 12

"Customers don't expect you to be perfect. They do expect you to fix things when they go wrong."

–Donald Porter

Brian's Take:

This isn't a license for incompetence. Incompetence and negligence aren't what Porter is talking about; he's talking about sincere mistakes and mishaps.

Hundreds of studies and anecdotes exist about customer-service failures that resulted in greater customer loyalty and delight because the issues were fixed in a timely and professional fashion.

Respond, repair and delight.

#CD365Day12

21

January 13

"Hire character. Train skill."

–Peter Schutz

Brian's Take:

Hire delightful people. Train them how to run the cash register!

#CD365Day13

January 14

"Kindness in words creates confidence. Kindness in thinking creates profoundness. Kindness in giving creates love."

–Lao Tzu

Brian's Take:

Kindness is at the root of amazing results.

Profound confident love...a.k.a. delight!

#CD365Day14

January 15

"People don't want to communicate with an organization or a computer. They want to talk to a real, live, responsive, responsible person who will listen and help them get satisfaction."

–Theo Michelson

Brian's Take:

Theo Michelson is on to something. Despite all the advances in technology, I've never heard anyone say, "I would rather reach the automated system versus a live person." When companies can't afford to put real people on the line to handle your complaint or challenge, it's pretty telling storyline about the lack of customer service and delight in today's marketplace.

What if companies focused on Customer Delight on all fronts? If we deliver Customer Delight in the field, we need fewer Customer-Delight reps to answer the phones, which means we could actually afford to staff properly for the "rare" customer complaint or challenge.

Customer Delight is a front-end decision with back-end impact.

#CD365Day15

January 16

"When you feel dog tired at night, it may be because you've growled all day long."

–Unknown

Brian's Take:

As humans, we're wired for efficiency. If our minds are always growling, our response begins to default to growling.

What kind of environment have you created for your employees? Have you removed the items that cause your employees to growl?

Don't let your employees get dog-tired growling at things you can change. Remember to create an environment where they can wag their tails.

Your dog-tired customers will appreciate the delight of your employees' tails wagging.

#CD365Day16

January 17

"To be successful, you have to have your heart in your business, and your business in your heart."

–Thomas J. Watson

Brian's Take:

When you arrive at work, do you check your heart at security or is it part of your toolkit for delighting your customers?

#CD365Day17

January 18

The chorus from the song "Tubthumping"

–Chumbawamba

Brian's Take:

If I haven't already infected you with an earworm by simply referencing the chorus of Chumbawamba's anthem for customer-service professionals, then please stop reading this book and join the rest of the infected world and follow this link. (Don't forget to come back and finish the book.)

Link: http://bit.ly/cd365chumba

Sometimes, you just need a silly song to keep you smiling. I won't deny that working in customer service can be challenging. I recommend you find a theme song for your customer-service team that keeps them motivated.

I suspect the members of Chumbawamba had some regular jobs on their way to musical success. Thank God, they got up again!

#CD365Day18

January 19

"Strive not to be a success, but rather to be of value."

–Albert Einstein

Brian's Take:

I wonder why Einstein didn't convert this to an equation: Energy + Value = Success.

Success happens to be a byproduct—not a destination—of creating value. When it comes to customer service, don't fret; many equations create Customer Delight.

I encourage you to take the time to create your own formulas for success, value and delight in your business.

#CD365Day19

January 20

"Approachability is about availability. Personally AND physically. It's not just about an open door policy, it's about an open mind policy."

–Scott Ginsberg, That Guy with a Nametag

Brian's Take:

Scott Ginsberg is famous for wearing a nametag everywhere he goes. He believes that a nametag is one of the first steps in making people comfortable and in making you approachable.

This concept is very much about the physical aspect of approachability, but we all know that the welcome mat does not always say "Welcome" to your clients. I've been to plenty of establishments with a welcome mat but an unwelcoming attendant. They don't need to say anything—I feel it.

Take Scott's approach of an open mind and add an open heart. Don't be surprised as this will cause the door to Customer Delight to swing wide open!

#CD365Day20

January 21

"Defeat is not bitter unless you swallow it."

–Joe Clark

Brian's Take:

Defeat is like wearing a blindfold in a rose garden. If you believe your eyes, you might think you're in a black hole of despair. But the rose garden is still there, even though you can't see it.

Success in life and business is often right in front of us, but it's shaded by our own doubt, insecurities and poor attitude. Next time you're faced with a challenging customer, ask yourself, "Will I accept defeat or take off my blindfold and see de-light?"

Defeat is always a choice. Delight is always a choice.

#CD365Day21

January 22

"The only way of finding the limits of the possible is by going beyond them into the impossible."

–Arthur C. Clarke

Brian's Take:

I like to break down this quote in a different fashion. "Impossible" with an apostrophe and a press of the space bar becomes "I'm possible!"

When we believe in the "I'm possible," we get the possible.

Customers delight in the "I'm possible" customer-service professional.

#CD365Day22

January 23

"I love to tell stories. It's a delight for me."

–James Patterson

Brian's Take:

Stories are the secret weapon for creating Customer Delight.

When your business has a storyline that includes your customer, not just you and your employees, your business will flourish with an exponential appeal.

#CD365Day23

January 24

"Less is more."   -   "Less is a bore."

–Ludwig Mies van der Rohe   –Robert Venturi

Brian's Take:

I found it interesting that these two quotes were back-to-back when I was conducting research for this book. Both quotes are true when it comes to Customer Delight.

One of my favorite phrases from one of my mentors is "Both and."

Less is both a bore and more. Less can also be more or a bore. Yes, it's kind of a mind bend. Yes, people are a mind bend.

Customer Delight requires intuition and awareness because, sometimes, what you thought was delight may not be delight.

Delight in the dichotomy of life.

#CD365Day24

January 25

"Thousands of candles can be lighted from a single candle, and the life of the candle will not be shortened. Happiness never decreases by being shared."

–Buddha

Brian's Take:

Most everything in business has a cost, but sharing your joy is one thing that is free. In fact, it's renewable and multiplies the more you give it.

"De-light" of a single candle might be the best marketing plan.

#CD365Day25

January 26

"When people in stadiums do the Wave, it's the group-mind collective organism spontaneously organizing itself to express an emotion, pass time, and reflect the joy of seeing the rhythms of many as one, a visual rhyming or music in which everyone senses where the motion is going."

–Jerry Saltz

Brian's Take:

I think organizations with "cult-like" followings, such as Apple, Starbucks and sports teams, understand that delight increases when they create a collective experience with their customers.

Does the sports team have to spend any money on the Wave to allow its customers to experience delight? What ways does your product or service allow for your clients to connect emotionally with your product?

One Grande, Delightful, MacBook Pro, No Soy, Wave Latte ready for Brian!

#CD365Day26

January 27

"Proper Preparation Prevents Poor Performance."

–Nancy Bleeke

Brian's Take:

Do I need to say more?

These are the 5 P's for creating the big D: DELIGHT.

#CD365Day27

January 28

"Happiness... consists in giving, and in serving others."

–Henry Drummond

Brian's Take:

Customer delight, which is made up of giving and serving, is a great way to be part of creating happiness in the world.

Nothing wrong with being part of one of the world's most common desires!

#CD365Day28

January 29

"Be kind whenever possible. It is always possible."

–Dalai Lama

Brian's Take:

If the Dalai Lama says it's possible, then what is holding you back?

I believe the only thing between this quote being true and not true is the story that lives between your two ears. This quote is about changing your story.

Your customer's story is a direct reflection of the story you have in your head. I believe it is possible to delight every customer, at all times.

My story is now your story!

#CD365Day29

January 30

"A successful man is one who can lay a firm foundation with the bricks others have thrown at him."

–David Brinkley

Brian's Take:

I'd be lying if I didn't admit that I've had my fair share of days as a customer-service professional that included a few bricks thrown in my direction. I'm sure you have, too!

I'm not even going to sugarcoat this one. Expect it, live for it and build a foundation for success with your pile of bricks!

#CD365Day30

January 31

"Intelligence is nothing without delight."

–Paul Claudel

Brian's Take:

Customer service is nothing without delight. An even exchange is just that. It's only when we give more than we take that we also find delight, which is an oxymoron because then we get more in return.

Delight is a mysterious formula for success in life and business.

#CD365Day31

February

February 1

"Luck is what happens when preparation meets opportunity."

–Seneca the Younger

Brian's Take:

Which is the same place where satisfaction meets delight: Preparation.

#CD365Day32

February 2

"Statistics suggest that when customers complain, business owners and managers ought to get excited about it. The complaining customer represents a huge opportunity for more business."

–Zig Ziglar

Brian's Take:

Complaints are like death and taxes—they're inevitable—so it's best to have a Delight Plan in place for when they occur.

If every business owner took my advice in regards to complaints, then death, taxes and delight would be three things you could count on in life.

#CD365Day33

February 3

"Nature is pleased with simplicity."

–Isaac Newton

Brian's Take:

Row, row, row your boat, gently down the stream, merrily, merrily, merrily, life is but a dream.

When you're crafting your customer experience, ask yourself "Which way is my customer's stream flowing?"

Nature often provides clues to creating unique and delightful customer experiences.

The flow is the quickest path to delight.

#CD365Day34

February 4

"If you neglect your art for one day it will neglect you for two."

–Chinese Proverb

Brian's Take:

You can climb only so high in the eyes of your client, but you can fall off the cliff in an instant.

Neglect your client once, your client might neglect you forever.

Customer Delight requires daily attention. Even a hint of neglect can put a great relationship on the rocks.

Steady as she goes!

#CD365Day35

February 5

"When something is new to us, we treat it as an experience. We feel that our senses are awake and clear. We are alive."

–Jasper Johns

Brian's Take:

Awake, clear and alive: Now that sounds like a delightful customer experience.

How are you keeping your customer-service experience fresh, so your customers feel the rush of being awake and clear?

Billy Crystal is famous for saying, "You look marvelous," in his comedy skits. Start telling your customers, "You look marvelous," and see what kind of smiles you get.

Delight!

#CD365Day36

February 6

"Make your optimism come true."

–Christian D. Larson

Brian's Take:

Optimism is often mistaken for an attitude when it is actually an action.

If your optimism isn't congruent with your outcomes, I bet you aren't as optimistic as you think you are.

Here's my simple formula for creating optimism:

1) Ask yourself, "What are my options? And who can help me with my options?"

2) Take action on your options, and ask for help.

3) Take delight in the miracles you've created with your optimism!

#CD365Day37

February 7

"At times our own light goes out and is rekindled by a spark from another person. Each of us has cause to think with deep gratitude of those who have lighted the flame within us."

–Albert Scwheitzer

Brian's Take:

What an amazing thought: Our "de-light" goes out and is rekindled by others. And we, too, can rekindle de-light in others.

Have you ever contemplated the word "delight" as being "of the light"? Delight truly is a spark that can spread and change your business, change your world.

Have you ever considered that sometimes we get re-ignited by the flames we create in others?

#CD365Day38

February 8

"Our job is to make change. Our job is to connect to people, to interact with them in a way that leaves them better than we found them, more able to get where they'd like to go. Every time we waste that opportunity, every page or sentence that doesn't do enough to advance the cause is a waste."

–Seth Godin

Brian's Take:

The benefit of your product isn't always apparent. Our services are much more than we could ever imagine. A ballroom is a place to raise money to cure cancer. A car provides transportation to find new customers. The gym keeps me healthy, so I can be available for my family.

Consider the ultimate benefits of your product or service, and you'll never need to worry about wasting an opportunity. Because you'll be changed, your only option is to change others.

#CD365Day39

February 9

"The customer's perception is your reality."

–Kate Zabriskie

Brian's Take:

Your ability to perceive your customer's reality is directly proportional to your ability to deliver Customer Delight.

#CD365Day40

February 10

"Where the senses fail us, reason must step in."

–Galileo Galilei

Brian's Take:

Reason is not the place to be when it comes to Customer Delight. We're not reasonable and rational beings, so why are you building your customer-service experience around rational decisions?

I use the bank with treats for my dog at the drive-thru and the hair salon that gives suckers to my daughter. Suckers might be the worst giveaway at a hair salon (think of all the hair), but my daughter always wants to go with me when I get a haircut.

Suckers and doggy treats. Simple delights can be the big difference.

#CD365Day41

February 11

"I won't complain. I just won't come back."

–Brown & Williamson tobacco ad

Brian's Take:

The scary thing about delivering less than exceptional customer service is that disappointed customers don't always tell you they won't come back. They just move on.

The alternative is to deliver something special and have your customers invite their friends to join them at your place of business.

Your choice.

#CD365Day42

February 12

"We awaken in others the same attitude of mind we hold toward them."

–Elbert Hubbard

Brian's Take:

Well, that's awkward. If you have a bad attitude about your customers, you activate that attitude in them.

Customer Delight can be as simple as you changing your attitude.

Awaken delight.

#CD365Day43

February 13

"The way to a customer's heart is much more than a loyalty program. Making customer evangelists is about creating experiences worth talking about."

–Valeria Maltoni

Brian's Take:

It might be easy to miss the most important words in Valeria Maltoni's quote. "Loyalty," "evangelism" and "customer experience" are all important facets of great customer service. But the customer's heart is often an overlooked factor when creating a great customer experience.

When you can find a way to touch a customer's heart, your business will thrive.

Service is a surface experience. Delight is a matter of the heart.

#CD365Day44

February 14

"Being on par in terms of price and quality only gets you into the game. Service wins the game."

–Tony Allesandra

Brian's Take:

Delight trumps service, price and quality, but that doesn't mean you should ignore them.

In fact, service, price and quality with a dash of delight is the recipe for referrals. And a referral recipe is the ultimate business plan.

#CD365Day45

February 15

"Although fate presents the circumstances, how you react depends on your character."

–Anonymous

Brian's Take:

If you only take away one thing from this book, know that circumstances do not drive the creation of delight.

Delight is a choice or an action that can create circumstances, but delight isn't dictated by the circumstances.

Make delight the circumstance, and you will change the world forever.

#CD365Day46

February 16

"Clutter and confusion are failures of design, not attributes of information."

–Edward Tufte

Brian's Take:

I can only think of Steve Jobs and Apple when I read this quote.

One button on the iPhone, the most powerful tool ever known to man, gets me where I need to go. Yes, I just said the iPhone is the most powerful tool ever known to man, and it has one-button navigation.

I challenge you to consider how you can channel Steve Jobs in your customer experience.

Apple's success wasn't a fluke. One small button for an iPhone, one giant leap for delight.

#CD365Day47

February 17

"Those three things—autonomy, complexity and a connection between effort and reward—are, most people will agree, the three qualities that work has to have if it is to be satisfying."

–Malcom Gladwell

Brian's Take:

As a business owner, manager or leader, you must always remember it's your responsibility to create the environment for your success in business.

When you "game" the system by providing a forum for your employees to find autonomy, complexity and connection, you create satisfied employees who create delighted customers.

Remember, it's your responsibility.

#CD365Day48

February 18

"Our success in life is directly related to the quantity and quality of service we give."

–Unknown

Brian's Take:

If you could give away something and get it back, why would you hang on to it?

If you embrace the principle of reciprocity—getting what you give—you can shift from a life of finite to infinite.

#CD365Day49

February 19

"The minute you learn how to give, is the minute you become successful."

–Hugh MacLeod

Brian's Take:

So many companies forget about "giving" as a strategy for giving. I know, that sentence is a bit of a mind-bender, because most people give to get, and your customers can see right through when you're giving to get. But if you can somehow truly give, the get is assured.

It's a fine line. As I like to say, it's a "mind-f~ck."

"For-getting" is a dead end, but "for-giving" is delightful!

#CD365Day50

February 20

"Don't put a limit on what can be accomplished."

–Christopher Reeve

Brian's Take:

I almost passed on this quote. I wondered when Christopher Reeve first shared this quote. Was it before or after he lost his ability to move his arms and legs, to breathe on his own, to feed himself, to do just about anything?

What I find powerful in his statement is no matter how dire our physical circumstances in life, we still have access to our most powerful tools—our mind and spirit. A great mind and spirit can do much more for the world than a great physical being.

If Reeve can have the courage to put this kind of statement out into the world, I'm pretty sure most of us have no excuses when it comes to creating delight for ourselves and our customers.

#CD365Day51

February 21

"A business has to be involving, it has to be fun, and it has to exercise your creative instincts."

–Sir Richard Branson

Brian's Take:

Unfortunately, I have crossed paths with businesses that don't hit even one of Branson's edicts.

When you come across a quote like this, the most important thing to do is to flip it into questions.

"How does my business create involvement, fun and creative expression for my employees and customers? Where do we fall short in these areas? Where are we not excelling? What are we going to do to improve in these areas?"

#CD365Day52

February 22

"Beauty without expression is boring."

–Ralph Waldo Emerson

Brian's Take:

Have you ever experienced a product or service that, on paper, is perfect but actually leaves you feeling that something is missing?

That's the distinction between customer satisfaction and customer delight.

On paper, your product quality may be 10 out of 10. But as a complete customer experience, your product might only register as a five because it lacks a connection with the heart.

If Emerson were talking about customer service instead of beauty he might say that customer service without delight is boring.

#CD365Day53

February 23

"Customers perceive service in their own unique, idiosyncratic, emotional, irrational, end-of-the-day, and totally human terms. Perception is all there is!"

–Tom Peters

Brian's Take:

The truth is that no exact, slam-dunk method exists for creating an exceptional customer experience.

Humans are both rational and irrational beings, which means you must always be in the moment with your customers. And that means not all of your customer interactions will lead to delight.

But I bet the cards are stacked in your favor when you stay present to your customer's state of being. Your deal!

#CD365Day54

February 24

"B, I, N, G, O and Bingo was his name-oh!"

–Ella Monahan singing William Swords' song

Brian's Take:

When my daughter was five years old, she belted out this song during one of my writing sessions. Sometimes delight is as simple as a song about a dog named Bingo. Something light, something delight and Bingo was his name OH!

Life and business doesn't need to be so serious. BINGO!

#CD365Day55

February 25

"Be a light, not a judge. Be a model, not a critic."

–Stephen Covey

Brian's Take:

A few years ago, I made a shift when it came to being a customer. For many years, I was a bit arrogant, critiquing and judging how companies and organizations delivered their products.

After a few particularly bad weeks at work, I realized that the business of serving people can be demanding, which is the understatement of the day. I decided to start seeing the people serving me as people instead of servants. My heart opened a bit, and I realized that I must be for the delight of the customer and the server.

That small opening created space for me to write this book.

Critique doesn't bring you closer to delight. Delight begets delight.

#CD365Day56

February 26

"There is only one boss. The customer. And he can fire everybody in the company from the chairman on down, simply by spending his money somewhere else."

–Sam Walton

Brian's Take:

In his statement, Sam Walton includes everyone in the company from the chairman to the front line, which is an important reminder of the incredible responsibility entrusted to our frontline staff.

When we don't delight our customers, we all risk losing our financial stability. Customer Delight might be the difference between being homeless or prosperous.

#CD365Day57

February 27

"The moment you stop asking questions you're on the path to obsolescence."

–Robin Sharma

Brian's Take:

One of the steps of process improvement is to reflect and review your work. Improving your customer experience might be as simple as asking yourself: "How can I expand the delight of my customers?" You can also take it a step further and ask your clients about what brings them delight.

Who, what, when, where and why your delight factor and see how it impacts your bottom line.

#CD365Day58

February 28

"Offer additional products that will allow your customers to continue to purchase your experience."

–Scott Ginsberg, That Guy with a Nametag

Brian's Take:

Why did I pay $89 for a Coca-Cola rugby shirt in 1987? Because Coke created something more than a cola; they created an American icon.

OK, if your product sucks, don't try to sell me your logo shirt, but if you have a great product, I might be willing to pay for a small billboard called a T-shirt.

Hey, to be clear, this is not about T-shirts. This is about extending your customers' experience beyond your product. Hint: This is called creating delight.

#CD365Day59

February 29

"SURPRISE! This book should really be titled Customer Delight 366."

–Brian Monahan

Brian's Take:

One of the greatest techniques you can add to your approach to customer delight is the element of SURPRISE. A surprise, an unexpected prize, is a great way to create memorable customer experiences.

In honor of leap year, I reached out to some of my favorite peeps and they agreed to provide you with some great surprises.

Visit this link to get your SURPRISE. http://www.customerdelight365.com/surprise

#CD365Day366

March

March 1

"It's not knowing what to do, it's doing what you know."

–Tony Robbins

Brian's Take:

There's absolutely no way to anticipate every situation or challenge in life and business. What we can do is prepare ourselves technically, emotionally and spiritually to be ready for when challenges arrive. Your customers will appreciate your confidence and courage.

When I find myself in a challenging situation with no clear path, I remind myself that there isn't a right answer. I ask myself, based on what I know and what information is available to me, how best should I proceed.

Proceeding frequently is the difference between customer dissatisfaction and customer delight. Customers often will forgive honest mistakes, but they don't forgive inaction.

Proceed to delight.

#CD365Day60

March 2

"Customer service is the experience we deliver to our customer. It's the promise we keep to the customer. It's how we follow through for the customer. It's how we make them feel when they do business with us."

–Shep Hyken

Brian's Take:

Customer Delight is when you can put all these things together on a consistent basis for your customers. Is your company a "one-hit wonder" or do your customers buy your "greatest hits" albums?

When crafting an awesome customer experience, consider the album model. String together a common theme of delightful experiences (songs) in the delivery of your product and service.

#CD365Day61

March 3

"If your business plan depends on suddenly being 'discovered' by some big shot, your plan will probably fail. Nobody suddenly discovers anything. Things are made slowly and in pain."

–Hugh MacLeod

Brian's Take:

Unless your product is for the big shots, forget about the big shots. Do your work daily, improve your work daily, and create delight daily. You will be the big shot.

Go!

#CD365Day62

March 4

"I don't like that man. I must get to know him better."

–Abraham Lincoln

Brian's Take:

Interestingly, in many companies, the customer becomes an enemy of the organization. It's an understandable scenario, but this is very dangerous territory.

If you notice you aren't in love with your customers, it's time to get to know your customers. It's easy to hate a customer; it's hard not to love a person. Personal connection is almost always the answer.

When we know our customers, we can be our customers. When we are one with our customers, the only outcome is delight.

#CD365Day63

March 5

"Being able to touch so many people through my businesses and make money while doing it, is a huge blessing."

–Magic Johnson

Brian's Take:

When you're in the groove of creating Customer Delight, a funny thing happens: You realize that you're getting more than you're giving.

Delight is perpetual, a self-fulfilling prophecy.

#CD365Day64

March 6

"Stop chasing the money and start chasing the passion."

–Tony Hsieh

Brian's Take:

It's easy to get distracted with the money reference in this quote, but the real power in this message is about moving toward passion.

Most of us mistake the word "passion" for a feeling of elation, so we never find true passion. True passion actually includes an element of pain. You might need to move toward a little bit of pain to find delight. I know, it's a mind-bender.

Delight in the passion of serving your customers. The money will then chase you.

#CD365Day65

March 7

"The sun shines and warms and lights us and we have no curiosity to know why this is so; but we ask the reason of all evil, of pain, and hunger, and mosquitoes and silly people."

–Ralph Waldo Emerson

Brian's Take:

This book comes from me asking the question, "What is Customer Delight?"

Are you asking the right questions for your business and customers? It's way too easy to ask how we can simply overcome life's challenges and annoyances.

It's another thing to ask: "Why is there Customer Delight and how can I create it?"

#CD365Day66

March 8

"While we cannot always choose what happens to us, we can choose our responses."

–Stephen Covey

Brian's Take:

Stephen Covey sums up everything you need to know about creating a great customer experience. If you can get your head around the idea that "Sh^t happens," you can be ready with the toilet paper.

Great organizations plan for their response to challenges. Interesting. Is it really a challenge if it was part of the plan? So delightful.

#CD365Day67

March 9

"Accountability breeds response-ability."

–Stephen Covey

Brian's Take:

We established that "Sh^t happens" in yesterday's passage, and we know that great organizations plan to respond to challenges.

It's fair to say we are both accountable and response-able for the outcome. Customers love when we are accountable.

Response-ability breeds delight-ability.

CD365Day68

March 10

"Weakness of attitude becomes weakness of character."

–Albert Einstein

Brian's Take:

A bad attitude is like rust on your bumper. At first, it's a small blemish. But left unattended, it will eventually compromise the integrity of your vehicle. If the integrity of your company is compromised, then you can pretty much kiss your business goodbye.

A positive attitude is akin to waxing and polishing your car. A polished car glistens in de-light.

#CD365Day69

March 11

"All it takes is one idea to solve an impossible problem."

–Robert H. Shuller

Brian's Take:

What Robert H. Shuller fails to mention is it often takes hundreds of wrong ideas to solve an impossible problem. The real problem is most organizations fail to act on the one or many great ideas.

Ideas in potential are simply accomplices to the problem. You must act on your many great ideas to find the one idea that solves the impossible problem.

If you're reading this thinking, "What in the world does this have to do with Customer Delight?" then you might want to find a new job. Customer Delight is the pursuit of overcoming the impossible problem: delighting people!

This is my great idea: . Thanks for joining me on this journey. By the way, I have a number of other ideas that you didn't notice before this "one idea."

#CD365Day70

March 12

"All credibility, all good conscience, all evidence of truth come only from the senses."

–Friedrich Nietzsche

Brian's Take:

Your company's credibility also relies on the truth of the senses—third-party senses. Your customer is the ultimate authority on the credibility of your product or service.

Delight is the ideal third-party credibility, as it creates an environment for your customers to "go viral" with their delight in your product.

#CD365Day71

March 13

"I gotta have more cowbell."

–Christopher Walken

Brian's Take:

Christopher Walken's *Saturday Night Live* skit from 2000 is a parody of the VH-1 series "Behind the Music." The skit follows the real band Blue Oyster Cult and the fictional cowbell player Gene Frankle. Walken's character gives the band advice on their studio session of "Don't Fear the Reaper" and lays down one of the greatest Internet memes of all time: "Well, guess what! I've got a fever, and the only prescription is more cowbell!"

Although this is a parody, the truth is that sometimes delighting your customers is as simple as more cowbell. Maybe cowbell isn't the core of your product or service, but a little flourish can go a long way.

Dink, dink, dink!

#CD365Day72

March 14

"Be everywhere, do everything, and never fail to astonish the customer."

–Macy's motto

Brian's Take:

"Be everywhere, do everything" is the opposite of not seeing the forest because all you can see is trees.

Winning companies recognize that they provide more than just the obvious transactions. A hotel might be selling a bed to sleep in, but it's allowing its customers to visit family or conduct business. Hotels aren't in the business of sleep but in the business of making it easier for their guests to experience delight away from home.

The "never fail" part of the equation is asking the question: "What else does my customer need with my product or service to experience delight?"

#CD365Day73

March 15

"Customers have lots of choices. When they choose you, be glad."

–Bill Leinweber

Brian's Take:

Better yet, throw a party!

#CD365Day74

March 16

"Be amused with yourself."

–Brian Monahan

Brian's Take:

If you don't have a good feeling about you, you surely can't share it with others.

A "muse" is a guiding spirit or source of inspiration. "Amuse" is defined as to laugh or give pleasure. It is my vision that *Customer Delight 365* will be the guiding spirit for creating Customer Delight muses around the world.

Will you amuse me by joining me on this journey?

#CD365Day75

March 17

"Nobody cares how much you know, until they know how much you care."

–Theodore Roosevelt

Brian's Take:

Why are you starting your sales pitch with information about your services? Start with what, how and why you do what you do for your customers and potential customers.

Try this the next time you're pitching a customer: "At XYZ Company, we care about ..."

Hint, if your dot, dot, dot is about cashing checks, you're on the wrong track.

#CD365Day76

March 18

"Successful people are the ones who are breaking the rules."

–Seth Godin

Brian's Take:

Customer Delight is about breaking the rules.

You are such a bad boy, bad girl, you Rule Breaker!

#CD365Day77

March 19

"We often take for granted the very things that most deserve our gratitude."

–Cynthia Ozick

Brian's Take:

Don't make this mistake when it comes to your customers. It's easy to forget that our clients hire us to take away their challenges and obstacles. This means that you should expect a certain amount of challenge with every customer. This can lead to frustration and negligence.

Delight in your daily challenge.

#CD365Day78

March 20

"The attitude is very important. Because, your behavior radiates how you feel."

–Lou Ferrigno

Brian's Take:

I think it's just wonderful to have The Incredible Hulk talking about radiating feelings. If anyone should know how radiation affects the way others experience us, it would be The Hulk.

Consider your reading of this book as my version of radiating you with extreme delight. Now whenever you find yourself inflamed by a customer, instead of radiating green with anger, you will shine bright with delight.

#CD365Day79

March 21

"There is no such thing as an empty space or an empty time. There is always something to see, something to hear. In fact, try as we may to make a silence, we cannot."

–John Cage

Brian's Take:

There's no such thing as a meaningless transaction. Every moment is an opportunity to connect. Try as we may, we can't disconnect, but we can miss-connect.

Hint: When a person is in front of you, remember: Connect.

#CD365Day80

March 22

"There are no menial jobs, only menial attitudes."

–William J. Brennan, Jr.

Brian's Take:

One of the biggest mistakes companies make is not connecting employees with a common vision. When employees lack vision, they're left to their own devices when it comes to creating a great customer experience.

A company focused on Customer Delight understands that all of the organization's employees and functions must be valued and tied together, otherwise Customer Delight is left to chance.

Chance is not a recipe for delight.

#CD365Day81

March 23

"Don't find fault. Find a remedy."

–Henry Ford

Brian's Take:

Finding fault is always the booby prize in life and business. Remedy is the path to delight and success.

But what about when you screw up? Shouldn't you accept fault? I say, accept "responsibility," which is a much more powerful concept rooted in the word "response."

Response + remedy is a formula for life-long customers.

#CD365Day82

March 24

"More business is lost every year through neglect than through any other cause."

–Rose Kennedy

Brian's Take:

Neglect is the antithesis of delight; it's the rusting of your customer relationship. A customer relationship covered in rust will eventually dissolve.

How are you polishing your customer relationships? Delight is a great polishing agent.

#CD365Day83

March 25

"To hell with circumstances; I create opportunities."

–Bruce Lee

Brian's Take:

Circumstances are a constant in life and customer service, but all too often, circumstances are misappropriated as reasons.

Reasons are the opposite of delight when it comes to creating happy customers. One of my favorite concepts is that you can either have reasons (circumstances) or you can have results (delight).

Which will you serve to your customer?

#CD365Day84

March 26

"People are definitely a company's greatest asset. It doesn't make any difference whether the product is cars or cosmetics. A company is only as good as the people it keeps."

–Mary Kay Ash

Brian's Take:

It's easy to think that the point of this quote is for you to hire good people, which is important. But even more important is, "How do you *keep* good people?"

Delighting your employees is a prerequisite for delighting your customers.

#CD365Day85

March 27

"Your attitude, not your aptitude, will determine your altitude."

–Zig Ziglar

Brian's Take:

Zig Ziglar might be the all-time expert on the impact of attitude in sales and customer service. Occasionally, someone with aptitude will rise to the top of their profession, but I would bet on someone with the right attitude nine out of 10 times when it comes to success in life and business.

If attitude is the determining factor for your success in life, then you really don't have an excuse. Attitude is the one thing we have the most control over.

Your positive attitude will become your customer's delight.

#CD365Day86

March 28

"Nordstrom's Rules for Employees: Rule #1: Use your good judgment in all situations. There are no additional rules."

–Nordstrom's Employee Rules

Brian's Take:

You can approach implementing this rule for your company in a couple of ways. One way is through training. The easier way is to hire people who possess good judgment.

Customer Delight Rule #1: Hire customer-service professionals who possess good judgment. Now you don't need rules.

#CD365Day87

March 29

"Delight is the miracle of optimistic action."

–Brian Monahan

Brian's Take:

Writing this book has been quite a journey for me; lessons and insights are around every corner. While playing with a quote about optimism, I came up with this concept: Optimism + Action = Delightful Miracles.

My insight for this quote is not so much about the quote but about the formula. If you take the time to dig into creating a formula for creating delight for your customers, you'll become more effective at delivering it on a regular basis.

For example: Connect with the customer in under 5 seconds of entering the store + A product standard = Delight Created.

You can even do this for other aspects of your business: Blank + Blank = Profit Delight.

#CD365Day88

March 30

"We don't want to push our ideas on to customers, we simply want to make what they want."

–Laura Ashley

Brian's Take:

This might be the greatest relationship advice I've ever gotten. The best relationships are about helping the other party get what they want—not selling them what you want.

This aligns perfectly with the underpinnings of *Customer Delight 365*. Customer Delight starts with great customer relationships.

#CD365Day89

March 31

"Things turn out best for the people who make the best out of the way things turn out."

–John Wooden

Brian's Take:

In this book, we've covered this topic from a few different angles, reinforcing the golden rule of customer service: You can't always control the circumstances, but you can control your response to the circumstances.

Your customers are human, and most will recognize you cannot control the circumstance. But all customers know you have a choice on how your respond to their challenge.

Make the best of your customer's challenges. Make delight.

#CD365Day90

The Delightful Sting

Majestic overlooks, red rocks and a place called Garden of the Gods are some of the delightful sights you expect if you travel to Colorado Springs, an oasis in the high desert of the Rocky Mountains outside of Denver.

While I was writing this book, I visited this sanctuary in Colorado Springs: The Broadmoor Hotel and Resort. Its amenities and awards include five stars, five diamonds, 18 restaurants, a polo field, golf courses, spas and much more. It's the ultimate in luxury.

As I mentioned earlier, I am in the audio visual and production industry, and my work takes me to the finest facilities all over the world. With hundreds of hotel stays under my belt, I can say that The Broadmoor is in my top three. During my trip, I was reviewing an event for a future customer and had a break before dinner. It was a relatively short break, so a round of 18 or even nine holes wasn't going to fit into the schedule. I decided to walk the grounds, and I stumbled upon one of the 18 restaurants on the property.

It was an "old" English tavern, which isn't all that unique today. Hundreds of chains around the U.S tout their version of an English pub with bangers and mash, woody bars and thick beer. When I entered the bar, it was midafternoon on a bright August day, making it hard for my eyes to adjust to the dim tavern lighting. I was alone, and I sauntered up to the bar.

I asked for a menu. I looked it over and quickly became excited: They featured soft-pretzel sticks. Being a bit of a carb addict, my belly began to grumble with anticipation.

Not much of a drinker, I was scouring the beer list for a hard cider to go with my pretzel delights. If this was the end of my story, the pretzel sticks and cheese dip would've been worth the trip, but this story continues.

As the bartender approached me, she had her head down, looking at what I thought was a notebook or banquet check. I then saw her pull back her arm and flick her wrist like Nolan Ryan. Thud! Something had hit me in the chest! I about lost my mind. I was thinking, What the hell? What in the world did this bartender just throw at me? Was it a piece of ice? A shot glass? And why was she throwing it at me?

I peeked down at my chest, and to my surprise, I had been stung. I smiled from ear to ear. On my chest was a knitted bee, much like a Boy Scout badge or other knitted patch. It had a sticky back, and I am still trying to figure out how they can sling such a small item and have it hit you with the sticky side.

In case you're not familiar with the English tavern on the grounds of The Broadmoor Hotel and Resort, it's called the Golden Bee.

I immediately started asking questions and quickly found out that this wasn't a freak accident or a postal worker turned bartender. This was standard operating procedure at the Golden Bee. I learned that a bartender at the Golden Bee started the practice on his own in the 1960s, creating his own "bees" and tossing at his favorite customers. It was such a hit, the Golden Bee adopted it as their own and has been bankrolling the production of the bees ever since. Now, everyone who dines at the Golden Bee gets stung by the bartender or server upon arrival or soon after.

I learned from the manager that The Broadmoor/Golden Bee spends $30,000 to $40,000 per year on the custom bees, which includes special bees for holidays and events. The annual specialty bees have even become collector's items, and people come from all around just to be stung by the custom bees.

I love this story because who would think that something as simple as a sticky bee could be so delightful? Yes, the restaurant has great ambiance, great food and lots of adult beverages to attract a good customer base, but it's the sticky bees that make this place just delightful.

What are some simple and different ways you can make your business stand out from the competition?

Hint: If what you come up with is part of a feature list, it probably isn't what we're talking about. How can you learn from the Golden Bee and sting your customers with delight? Don't forget to look to your most-loved employees; they often have little customs and habits that they already share with your customers. Just BEE sure you give them the credit.

Key Takeaway: Delight isn't always about your product or service. Sometimes it's a unique experience that allows your employees and customers to connect on an emotional level.

April

April 1

"The difference between 'try' and 'triumph' is just a little 'umph.'"

–Marvin Phillips

Brian's Take:

I think it was Yoda who said there is "No try." "De-lights" are either on or they're off.

If you're crafty, build yourself a little box with a light switch, label the off position "Try" and the on position "Umph." When you take your post each day, flip the Delight Switch to Umph!

Can't wait to hear how this one turns out!

#CD365Day91

April 2

"A leader is one who knows the way, goes the way, and shows the way."

–John C. Maxwell

Brian's Take:

Leadership and customer service are almost the same thing. When we lead, we serve.

#CD365Day92

April 3

"Always do what you are afraid to do."

–Ralph Waldo Emerson

Brian's Take:

I don't think Emerson is talking about wrestling a tiger, but metaphorically speaking, we face tigers daily in life and business.

When it comes to standing out in business, a company that is willing to address the tough topics and overcome big obstacles is going to stand out from the crowd.

Counterintuitively, moving toward the challenges in life and business often leads to the greatest delight.

#CD365Day93

April 4

"Business is more exciting than any game."

–Lord Beaverbrook

Brian's Take:

Serving customers is an honor, not a chore. If serving your customer doesn't rank as one of your favorite things to do, find a new job.

#CD365Day94

April 5

"Practice isn't the thing you do once you're good. It's the thing you do that makes you good."

–Malcom Gladwell

Brian's Take:

Practice is our work; delight is our product.

I can get behind that kind of work.

#CD365Day95

April 6

"Ability is what you're capable of doing. Motivation determines what you do. Attitude determines how well you do it."

–Lou Holtz

Brian's Take:

This is a great quote for owners and managers. Lou Holtz is one of the greatest coaches of all time. What this quote fails to mention is that as a coach (owner and manager) or leader, your job is to boost your team in all these areas.

More ability, more motivation and better attitude are all friends of Customer Delight.

#CD365Day96

April 7

"The idea behind a dish—the delight and the surprise—makes a difference. Great literature surprises and delights, and provokes us. It isn't just 'Here's the facts—boy meets girl, boy loses girl, boy gets girl.' It's how you tell it."

–Nathan Myhrvold

Brian's Take:

This is where the vision and mission of your company intersect with your product or service. A delightful customer experience doesn't start at the transaction but at the heart of the matter.

What is your vision for your life and your business? Intersect that vision with your product and service, and notice how your customers respond differently.

It's a subtle difference, but people can sense when our work is connected to a greater purpose.

#CD365Day97

April 8

"If you're creative, if you can think independently, if you can articulate passion, if you can override the fear of being wrong, then your company needs you more than it ever did. And now your company can no longer afford to pretend that isn't the case."

–Hugh MacLeod

Brian's Take:

Same goes for your business as a whole. Think about this quote when you're hiring your team. Are you looking for sheep or creators?

Sheep may be consistent, but creators are delightful.

#CD365Day98

April 9

"Do your little bit of good where you are; it's those little bits of good put together that overwhelm the world."

–Desmond Tutu

Brian's Take:

I think it's easy to miss the meaning of this quote. It's not just about doing the little things, but doing the little things "where you are."

This is seeing the glass as half-full instead of half-empty. It's about owning the moment and acknowledging you have a choice. You can provide your customer a small taste of delight, or you can just go through the motions.

#CD365Day99

April 10

"No one can whistle a symphony. It takes a whole orchestra."

–H.E. Luccock

Brian's Take:

Just like a symphony, a well-orchestrated business or organization can create a delightful experience for its audience, its customer.

#CD365Day100

April 11

"Die when I may, I want it said by those who knew me best that I always plucked a thistle and planted a flower where I thought a flower would grow."

–Abraham Lincoln

Brian's Take:

This quote from Abraham Lincoln can interpretted a number of ways.

If you're a business owner, ask yourself if you have any employees who are thistle. If you do, replace them with flowers.

Or, as a customer-service professional, you can expect thistle in your days. It's your job to identify and remove the thistle for your customers. Sometimes, just the act of removing a "pain" for your customer is enough to grow delight.

Delight grows in the vacuum of plucked thistle.

#CD365Day101

April 12

"Learn to smile at every situation. See it as an opportunity to prove your strength and ability."

–Joe Brown

Brian's Take:

Smiling at every situation isn't akin to ignoring a situation. Smiling is about having a sense of confidence and purpose in your work.

Your clients can tell when you're in-touch with your strength as a customer-service professional. When customers sense your strength, trust is evoked.

Trust is the best friend of Customer Delight.

#CD365Day102

April 13

"Fishing is much more than fish. It is the great occasion when we may return to the fine simplicity of our forefathers."

–Herbert Hoover

Brian's Take:

It's important to remember that our lives are increasingly complex. Simplicity has become a luxury.

Simplicity is the art of slowing our minds and connecting with our source. A simple customer experience is good for the spirit of the world.

Luxurious and simply delightful!

#CD365Day103

April 14

"In *The Dip,* Seth Godin shares 7 reasons why you might fail to become the best in the world: 1.) You run out of time, 2.) you run out of money, 3.) you get scared, 4.) you're not serious about it, 5.) you lose interest or enthusiasm and settle for being mediocre, 6.) you focus on the short term instead of the long, 7.) you pick the wrong thing at which to be the best in the world."

-J.D. Meier on Seth Godin

Brian's Take:

Here are seven ways to create delight for your customers:

1) Create time for your customers.

2) Be profitable (so you can provide a viable product).

3) Overcome fear.

4) Get serious about delight, which (interestingly) isn't all that serious.

5) Settle for greatness.

6) Focus on your customer.

7) Pick the right attitude about whatever you choose to be best at in the world.

#CD365Day104

April 15

"Cock your hat—angles are attitudes."

–Frank Sinatra

Brian's Take:

Hollow pleasantries can be a barrier to Customer Delight. The world is full of copycats and lookalikes.

Sometimes the best path to Customer Delight involves a little edge. Think of it as a sharp cheese or spicy dish. Your customer experience should be "rememorable."

Start spreading the news!

#CD365Day105

April 16

"Don't take yourself too seriously. And don't be too serious about not taking yourself too seriously."

–Howard Ogden

Brian's Take:

One of my mentors says, "Seriousness is a disease."

Is your business a serious business? If so, you're doing it wrong.

I haven't found any formulas for delight that include the word "serious." Delight is joyful.

#CD365Day106

April 17

"'Have fun' is my message. Be silly. You're allowed to be silly. There's nothing wrong with it."

–Jimmy Fallon

Brian's Take:

Jimmy Fallon has more than proven the power in his words. He is not only silly but also uber successful. I've found fun to be a precursor to an open wallet.

#CD365Day107

April 18

"Biggest question: Isn't it really 'customer helping' rather than customer service? And wouldn't you deliver better service if you thought of it that way?"

–Jeffrey Gitomer

Brian's Take:

I think the problem with the term "customer service" is that it has an inherent association with work. When we're working, it's easy to forget about the delight factor.

Jeffrey Gitomer is a master of reframing customer service and the sales process. Take his advice, reframe your approach and help your customers experience delight.

#CD365Day108

April 19

"It comes from within."

–Stephen Covey

Brian's Take:

OK, we're going to stop this book in progress to deliver breaking news: Stephen Covey says, "It comes from within."

Stop and close your eyes for a moment. Ask yourself, "What would it take for me to connect with my own personal delight?"

Do that for yourself. If you can't find it in yourself, it's going to be hard to share it with your customers. Your customers can tell when you feel delighted inside.

We now resume the book in progress, *Customer Delight 365.*

#CD365Day109

April 20

"The best way to find yourself is to lose yourself in the service of others."

–Mahatma Gandhi

Brian's Take:

Talk about upping the ante. When we make our work about others, it can only make the world a better place.

It also has a direct correlation to increasing Customer Delight.

#CD365Day110

April 21

"Everyone is a genius. But if you judge a fish by its ability to climb a tree, it will spend its whole life believing it is stupid."

–Albert Einstein

Brian's Take:

Are you hiring fish or customer-service professionals?

"Holy mackerel!" might be good for Lent, but not so much for Customer Delight!

#CD365Day111

April 22

"To give real service you must add something which cannot be bought or measured with money, and that is sincerity and integrity."

–Douglas Adams

Brian's Take:

People spend their money with hopes of getting something they can't buy with money. That's a crazy dichotomy, but when you realize that your intangibles are worth more than your tangibles, you're ready to create Radical Delight.

I'm not quite sure what Radical Delight looks like, but it's an intriguing idea.

If you find it, drop me a line.

#CD365Day112

April 23

"People are illogical, unreasonable, and self-centered. Love them anyway."

–Kent M. Keith

Brian's Take:

Hint: People who are illogical, unreasonable and self-centered are your customers. Delight them anyway.

#CD365Day113

April 24

"The best customer-service professionals are also great customers."

–Brian Monahan

Brian's Take:

When I started writing this book, I took a really close look at how I treat customer-service professionals. Although I consider myself pretty laid back as a customer, I noticed that I can lose my cool when my expectations are not met.

It's really easy to dump my frustration on an "innocent" customer-service professional. Although their organization may have failed me, do they really deserve a dose of my rage?

Have you ever considered that what comes around goes around? The more you bring joy in the world as a customer or customer-service professional, the more delight there is in the world.

How are you showing up as a customer?

#CD365Day114

April 25

"A work of art is a world in itself reflecting senses and emotions of the artist's world."

–Hans Hofmann

Brian's Take:

Seth Godin also alludes to our work becoming meaningful when we approach it as art.

How are you approaching your customer experience? Is it a work of art or the cash register ringing?

#CD365Day115

April 26

"The goal as a company is to have customer service that is not just the best but legendary."

–Sam Walton

Brian's Take:

Sam Walton's quote ties in with the idea that if you're in the business of customer satisfaction, you're aiming too low. Customer Delight is the real target.

Today is a great time to decide what target you'll aim at. The best way to hit the target is to identify it and take aim.

#CD365Day116

April 27

"We are all instruments endowed with feeling and memory. Our senses are so many strings that are struck by surrounding objects and that also frequently strike themselves."

–Denis Diderot

Brian's Take:

Delight is very much like the concept of a tuning fork picking up on matching vibrations. If you don't feel delight in your heart, it's going to be hard for your customers to feel it, too.

Diderot also refers to the "many strings" we all have. Remember, each of your customers may feel delight in different ways. For example, one of my favorite strings of delight is surprise.

Striking the delight string requires you to seek new ways of delivering your product or service daily.

#CD365Day117

April 28

"If you do build a great experience, customers tell each other about that. Word of mouth is very powerful."

–Jeff Bezos

Brian's Take:

Amazon does 60 billion online transactions annually, and its founder and chief executive is talking about word of mouth.

I think I might listen to Bezos as it appears he is onto something, 60 billion somethings, that is.

What makes your customer experience delightful enough to get your customers talking?

#CD365Day118

April 29

"Whether success or failure: the truth of a life really has little to do with its quality. The quality of life is in proportion, always, to the capacity for delight. The capacity for delight is the gift of paying attention."

–May Sarton

Brian's Take:

In a conversation about Customer Delight, I doubt Sarton would advocate poor product quality but instead would advocate that we be awake to ourselves, and better yet, to our customers.

Pay attention to your customer, and they just might pay for your product.

#CD365Day119

April 30

"The first step in exceeding your customer's expectations is to know those expectations."

–Roy H. Williams

Brian's Take:

That's a novel idea: Know your customer's expectations.

This seems like an easy concept, but actually it requires more than just an intellectual knowledge of your customers' expectations—it requires that you care.

Do you care to exceed?

#CD365Day120

May

May 1

"Our attitude towards others determines their attitude towards us."

–Earl Nightingale

Brian's Take:

So you were telling me about your difficult customers? Tell me more about yourself.

#CD365Day121

May 2

"Nothing is interesting if you're not interested."

–Helen MacInness

Brian's Take:

This is one of the pillars of Customer Delight: It's easier to be interested than interesting.

Customers can't help but feel delighted when you're interested in them. If this doesn't come naturally, create a list of "interested" questions and conversation starters you can use to delight your customers.

Tell me about your day. Any plans for the holidays? Tell me about your children.

These aren't just examples: I'm really interested in hearing about you! Send me an email at brian@customerdelight365.com

#CD365Day122

May 3

"Most people have no clue what they want, and if you ask them, you'll get a lame answer. Most people don't know they want *Pretty Woman* or *Slumdog Millionaire*. They don't know they want Purple Cow or one of your killer articles. So if you want to have an impact, all you can do is lead. You can't ask."

–Seth Godin

Brian's Take:

Although it's important to listen to your customers, great innovations generally don't come from your customers.

Innovation, impact and Customer Delight is a synthesis of a true customer-service professional listening, noticing and acting on their customer's needs.

#CD365Day123

May 4

"Repeat business or behavior can be bribed. Loyalty has to be earned."

–Janet Robinson

Brian's Take:

Loyalty might be one of the most powerful concepts in business.

Jeffery Gitomer, a sales and business guru, wrote an entire book on the power of customer loyalty. His title sums up the concept: *Customer Satisfaction is Worthless, Customer Loyalty is Priceless.*

There's no secret sauce for creating customer loyalty. It requires you to care, connect and deliver—daily, in the moment and forever. It's a marriage of business and customer.

When both parties commit to each other, the sum is greater than its parts.

#CD365Day124

May 5

"People will forget what you said, people will forget what you did, but people will never forget how you made them feel."

–Maya Angelou

Brian's Take:

A high IQ is a great way to solve worldly problems, but EQ (emotional intelligence) is the language of delight.

Instead of taking a customer-training class, take a class on how people tick.

Do you feel what I am saying?

#CD365Day125

May 6

"Be Seth Godin, be Jeffrey Gitomer, be John Maxwell, be Tony Robbins. Be your great self."

-Brian Monahan

Brian's Take:

I'm a lifelong self-help junkie, always looking for the next and greatest book or idea. Looking to the gurus is fine, but if you want to become a unique organization or customer service-professional, eventually you must look inside.

Be your great self, it's always the best self.

Customers can get Seth Godin from Seth Godin and McDonald's from McDonald's.

What makes you unique? Bring it to the table and share it with your customers. Let them get you and get delight.

#CD365Day126

May 7

"Nothing is so contagious as enthusiasm."

–Samuel Taylor Coleridge

Brian's Take:

It's also been said that the only thing more contagious than enthusiasm, is the lack of enthusiasm.

Which will you spread?

#CD365Day127

May 8

"Most people spend more time and energy going around problems than in trying to solve them."

–Henry Ford

Brian's Take:

Hint: If it happens once, there's a good chance it can happen again.

Create a journal for your business. Track successes and challenges daily. Review daily and seek trends. Reinforce the positive. SOLVE your challenges.

Identifying challenges is just the tip of the iceberg. Solving them will transform your business and delight your customers.

#CD365Day128

May 9

"What you do with what you have is more important than what you have."

–Jim Rohn

Brian's Take:

I believe Jim Rohn's quote is rooted in gratitude. Gratitude is about being aware of what we have instead of what we don't have. It's the proverbial question of whether the glass is half-full or half-empty.

The only difference is that in a customer-service environment, it's not really our place to decide for our clients if the glass is half-full or half-empty. Our job is to find a way to fill it up with delight.

Delight-full!

#CD365Day129

May 10

"A great attitude does much more than turn on the lights in our worlds; it seems to magically connect us to all sorts of serendipitous opportunities that were somehow absent before the change."

–Earl Nightingale

Brian's Take:

Stop the presses! If you have even an ounce of belief in what Nightingale says about attitude, you're absolutely out of your mind if you don't do whatever it takes to have a great attitude.

A magical connection with serendipitous opportunities that were absent prior...

Can I get a "Woot-woot!?"

#CD365Day130

May 11

"We are involved in a life that passes understanding and our highest business is our daily life."

–John Cage

Brian's Take:

Our highest business is people; the transaction is a bonus and sometimes a byproduct or a distraction.

If we change our business culture to make our highest focus on creating connections and memorable experiences within our daily lives, the transactions will take care of themselves.

#CD365Day131

May 12

"Effort only fully releases its reward after a person refuses to quit."

–Napoleon Hill

Brian's Take:

How far are you willing to go for your client?

The reward for crossing the "no quit" threshold is a customer for life.

#CD365Day132

May 13

"When it's time to die, let us not discover that we have never lived."

–Henry David Thoreau

Brian's Take:

I know that is a heavy quote for a Customer Delight book, but I assure you that creating Customer Delight is very much about life and death.

I suspect if you spent your career creating delight, when it's time to die, you'll have discovered that you truly lived.

There's really no better way to spend your life than serving your fellow man.

#CD365Day133

May 14

"The only limits are, as always, those of vision."

–James Broughton

Brian's Take:

Customer Delight isn't a product of reaction but a product of someone's vision for a better customer experience.

Raise your gaze, raise your results.

#CD365Day134

May 15

"All business success rests on something labeled a sale, which at least momentarily weds company and customer."

–Tom Peters

Brian's Take:

I add that the closer this "sale" comes to creating delight, the longer the marriage.

Will you settle for a moment or create a lifelong relationship?

#CD365Day135

May 16

"A person's name is to him or her the sweetest and most important sound in any language."

–Dale Carnegie

Brian's Take:

The simplest way to change your customer's experience: Say their name, remember their name, and say their name.

#CD365Day136

May 17

"Face the simple fact before it comes involved. Solve the small problem before it becomes big."

–Lao Tzu

Brian's Take:

If you put spoiled milk back in the refrigerator, it might get cold, but it's still spoiled.

Creating Customer Delight requires timely attention to the challenges in your business process. A quick response to a challenging situation is often the difference between losing a customer and creating a loyal customer.

Reread that last sentence because there's more to it than meets the eye. A quick response to a customer challenge is actually an opportunity to create a loyal customer.

Loyalty is often won in the trenches.

#CD365Day137

May 18

"Where there's scarcity, there's value."

–Seth Godin

Brian's Take:

Seth Godin often discusses our "lizard brain" or the instinctual brain. Our lizard brain often leads us to conform.

In the pack, conforming might be a good thing. But in business, distinction is often the difference that leads to success.

As you craft your business model, consider how you can provide a scarce resource that brings delight.

#CD365Day138

May 19

"A hug is like a boomerang—you get it back right away."

–Bil Keane

Brian's Take:

Customer Delight is more easily described as "hugging" your customers.

Give delight, get delight.

It's not only energy efficient but also economically efficient!

#CD365Day139

May 20

"Disneyland is a work of love. We didn't go into Disneyland just with the idea of making money"

–Walt Disney

Brian's Take:

A business without love is like a person without a soul.

When you add "love" to your approach to customer service, your business becomes "alive."

Awaken your business with love. Delight is a byproduct of love.

#CD365Day140

May 21

"If the other person finishes their meal before you, you weren't listening enough. Or they eat too fast."

–Scott Ginsberg, That Guy with a Nametag

Brian's Take:

To be honest, I always finish my meal before my guest, but it's often about the latter: I eat too fast.

The most interesting guy in the room is the most interested guy in the room. It's counterintuitive, but when you show interest in others, they'll be far more interested in you than if you tried to entice them to be interested in you.

If I had to define how to create Customer Delight in 10 ideas or less, being interested vs. being interesting would make the cut, hands down.

#CD365Day141

May 22

"Delight is a mutual experience. Give it and you get to receive it."

–Brian Monahan

Brian's Take:

Delight is akin to a hug—the best way to get it is to give it.

Did I just quote myself? That might be against the law.

#CD365Day142

May 23

"Never treat your audience as customers, always as partners."

—Jimmy Stewart

Brian's Take:

Partnership is an amazing path to take in business. Partnership requires mutual investment, which is the most powerful type of business relationship. Investment requires risk with the hope for reward.

Is your product or service so amazing your customers are willing to risk that you can deliver Customer Delight?

#CD365Day143

May 24

"Sales without Customer Service is like stuffing money into a pocket full of holes."

–David Tooman

Brian's Take:

Sales plus Customer Delight is money in the bank.

#CD365Day144

May 25

"If we did the things we are capable of, we would literally astound ourselves."

–Thomas Edison

Brian's Take:

This quote isn't as straightforward as it might appear.

"If we did the things we are capable of..." This requires us to push our boundaries to exhaustion in order to recognize our true greatness.

How often are you leaving something on the table when taking care of your customers? They deserve your astounding greatness.

You are capable of extreme delight!

#CD365Day145

May 26

"Employees who are controlled cannot respond caringly, you need superior knowledge and real leadership, not management. Because of this we specifically developed a selection process for leaders; we don't hire managers."

–Horst Schulze

Brian's Take:

Schulze references "control" in many of his quotes about Ritz-Carlton employees.

"Control" is a heavy word, and I believe The Ritz-Carlton has stumbled on to a way to "de-lighten" the load on its employees by allowing them to connect with the customer and respond in a human way vs. responding with a controlled standard.

Standards are an easy way to hide out from the customer, where freedom to serve is a great way to generate delight.

#CD365Day146

May 27

"If you work just for money, you'll never make it, but if you love what you're doing and you always put the customer first, success will be yours."

–Ray Krock

Brian's Take:

Ray Krock essentially says that Customer Delight hinges on your delight, which is the ultimate win-win.

The customers get what they want, you're enjoying yourself, and you're making more money doing it. Which begs the question: If you love what you do, why isn't it called TGIM instead of TGIF?!

#CD365Day147

May 28

"Never doubt that a small group of thoughtful, committed citizens can change the world. Indeed, it's the only thing that ever has."

–Margaret Mead

Brian's Take:

Never doubt that you are the difference between winning or losing a customer.

You always have the opportunity to remind yourself that *you* are the linchpin to creating Customer Delight.

Thanks for joining my small group of customer-service professionals who are changing the world by exploring the power of *Customer Delight 365!*

#CD365Day148

May 29

"Empathy takes time, and efficiency is for things, not people."

–Stephen Covey

Brian's Take:

I highly recommend organizations become highly inefficient when it comes to completing tasks that create delight.

Many organizations have policies for billing for overtime labor. Do you have a policy for delivering your customers delight at time-and-a-half or double-time? Sounds silly, but take a step a back and ask yourself, "What would it look like to reward our customers with more delight?"

Hint: Surprising rewards are often worth way more than double time.

#CD365Day149

May 30

"To respond is positive, to react is negative."

–Zig Ziglar

Brian's Take:

On paper, responding and reacting seem to be almost the same thing. An experience or a circumstance occurs, and it creates another circumstance. I find the difference between a response and a reaction is that a reaction is automated while a response is pondered.

To create a response-centric customer experience, we must create space for ourselves or our employees. If we're always at capacity emotionally—as customer-service professionals—then we have no room to ponder the circumstances we must address.

A response-centric company creates emotional room for challenges. That room is the where the mind, body and spirit can meet the customer in the moment.

Save room for delight.

#CD365Day150

May 31

"In business, you can't be all sugar. Customers want value. Customers want substance. Customers want to take a few licks and then discover your Tootsie center."

–Scott Ginsberg, That Guy with a Nametag

Brian's Take:

Scott's message is much deeper than the Tootsie center he references. He isn't disregarding the sugar, which is a lot of what we've discussed in this book, but he is saying customers want something substantial to chew on. Customers also like a surprise, customers like anticipation.

How many licks does it take to get the center of your product's value proposition? Hopefully, it's so good the customer quits licking and start biting.

#CD365Day151

June

June 1

"People rarely succeed unless they have fun in what they are doing."

–Dale Carnegie

Brian's Take:

Fun is a game-changer for a business. If the employees are having fun, it likely means the customers are having fun...which means the owner is having fun—cashing checks!

Fun is for all. How do your create fun for your employees and customers?

#CD365Day152

June 2

Turn your face to the sun and the shadows fall behind you."

–Maori Proverb

Brian's Take:

Be the sun, and the shadows will fall behind your clients. So many of us look to our work to be the source when in fact we are the source, the sun.

Think about some of your favorite businesses; they often have someone who brings light to your life.

De-light is in you. Let it shine. Pun intended.

I'm smiling. I hope you are, too!

#CD365Day153

June 3

"Here is a simple but powerful rule—always give people more than what they expect to get."

–Nelson Boswell

Brian's Take:

At first glance, Nelson Boswell's quote seems quite simple but unsustainable for most businesses. Once you deliver more, then the customer wants more.

This is why Customer Delight isn't just happenstance.

Customer Delight requires you, as a company, to be very deliberate about your approach to customer service. In fact, often the difference between mere customer satisfaction and Customer Delight is a company that has a deliberate customer-service process.

#CD365Day154

June 4

"Thank your customer for complaining and mean it. Most will never bother to complain. They'll just walk away."

–Marilyn Suttle

Brian's Take:

Do you have a process for gathering feedback from your customers? It's easier than ever to post a survey online and beat the ones who won't complain to the punch, possibly saving a customer who otherwise would walk away.

What are you waiting for? Survey for delight!

#CD365Day155

June 5

"If you create something, whether it's a painting or a company, I think if you care about it, you have some obligation to go out and tell people about it."

–Daniel H. Pink

Brian's Take:

Pink's quote actually addresses two aspects of customer delight. First, it's OK to toot your horn. You have something great to share, so share it. Second, if you create an environment for your employees to create something they care about, they will want to share it.

I call that delightful marketing.

#CD365Day156

June 6

"Success isn't a result of spontaneous combustion. You must set yourself on fire."

–Arnold H. Glasow

Brian's Take:

What are your waiting for? Delight is in the heart of the beholder. Bring it forth into the world and watch it ignite in your customers.

Did someone yell "FIRE"?

#CD365Day157

June 7

"Winning is not a sometime thing; it's an all time thing. You don't win once in a while, you don't do things right once in a while, you do them right all the time. Winning is habit. Unfortunately, so is losing."

–Vince Lombardi

Brian's Take:

Customer Delight as a "sometime thing" is an odd choice for a business.

#CD365Day158

June 8

"A healthy attitude is contagious but don't wait to catch it from others. Be a carrier."

–Tom Stoppard

Brian's Take:

My goal for this book is to create an epidemic of Customer Delight. I suspect if you made it this far in the book, you are now infected with a healthy attitude of delight.

This is one epidemic where quarantining the infected isn't a good idea. Achoo!

#CD365Day159

June 9

"Kind words do not cost much. Yet they accomplish much."

–Blaise Pascal

Brian's Take:

In most cases, kind words cost nothing. Take an inventory of kind words and share them with your team. Have a competition and see who can use the most kind words in a day, with each other and with your customers.

If you and your customers aren't smiling by using this technique, I will refund in full the money you spent on kind words!

#CD365Day160

June 10

"It is those who are successful, in other words, who are most likely to be given the kinds of special opportunities that lead to further success."

–Malcom Gladwell

Brian's Take:

Hint: All systems in life are gamed. Whether it's success or failure, or frustration or delight. Whatever your status quo, you will get more of it.

Fair or not, it's a reality of life. If you can find a way to harness creating delight for your customers, you will likely be afforded the opportunity to do it again. Awesome!

#CD365Day161

June 11

"Wag more. Bark less."

–Bumper Sticker

Brian's Take:

Man's best friend is a great resource for insights in customer service. Next time a customer walks through the door, imagine yourself approaching your customer as a dog (metaphorically, of course). Your smile, your voice inflection, your handshake—or better yet, a hug—are all akin to wagging your tail.

Don't ever become too familiar with your customers. Get excited each and every time they enter your business. In fact, your customers are a lot like dogs, too. Be sure you have some "treats" for your customers. They will wag their tails with delight.

#CD365Day162

June 12

"Hell, there are no rules here—we're trying to accomplish something."

–Thomas Edison

Brian's Take:

The only real rule to creating Customer Delight is, "Your customer rules!"

Next time you have a challenge serving a customer, break the rules and err on an outcome of Customer Delight. I promise you it will pay off big!

#CD365Day163

June 13

"Start where you are. Use what you have. Do what you can."

–Arthur Ashe

Brian's Take:

We all have so much more to offer than we can ever imagine. Build on what you have, because it's the only foundation you can build on.

Unfortunately, most mistake digging a hole as being the same thing as being in a hole. If your company can't afford postage for thank-you cards, try saying "thank you" in person. Fill your hole with gravel until you can afford concrete.

#CD365Day164

June 14

"I would add that the closer this 'sale' comes to creating delight...the longer the marriage. Will you settle for a moment or create a lifelong relationship?"

—Jerry Fritz

Brian's Take:

Marriage is a great analogy for creating lifelong customers. If you go into a marriage with the plans of winning in the moment, your marriage will last a moment. If you go into marriage giving of your heart, you're destined for a long and prosperous relationship.

Customer Delight is pretty much the same as a marriage. It's about being all in with the customer.

#CD365Day165

June 15

"There are no traffic jams along the extra mile."

–Roger Staubach

Brian's Take:

The extra mile is where you gain momentum as a customer-service professional.

You'll find that when you go the extra mile to delight your clients, you will stand out because so few others are on that road.

#CD365Day166

June 16

"Any intelligent fool can make things bigger, more complex, and more violent. It takes a touch of genius— and a lot of courage—to move in the opposite direction."

–E. F. Schumacher

Brian's Take:

Shumacher's take on complexity is interesting. "Violent" is a strong description if you consider making your product more complex. Heed his warning the next time you decide to complicate the process for your customers to do business with you.

He also mentions that the opposite direction requires courage. It seems that creating delight would be an easy task, but in today's cynical world, it can feel risky to serve delight. But as with many risks, there is great reward. The best part is it is a reciprocal reward.

Delight is for the giver and the receiver.

#CD365Day167

June 17

"Trust: The reputation of a thousand years may be undermined by the conduct of one hour."

–Japanese Proverb

Brian's Take:

I train my employees with a simple business formula: You can never be ten up or even one up with a customer. At best, you are even.

You can't save up your good deeds in business. You must deliver daily. Warning: You might find yourself ten down with just a slight mess up.

Enjoy the even, because it's dangerous to think you are one up on the customer.

#CD365Day168

June 18

"I like to listen. I have learned a great deal from listening carefully. Most people never listen."

–Ernest Hemingway

Brian's Take:

Creating delight will often put you in the minority, which is actually a great place to be.

Hemingway provides a clue for creating delight. Listening is rare. When done with sincerity, it's at the core of creating great customer relationships.

#CD365Day169

June 19

"A discovery is said to be an accident meeting a prepared mind."

–Albert Szent-Gyorgyi

Brian's Take:

Delight is said to be a challenge facing a prepared mind.

Delight is rarely an accident. You must be ready to serve on the good days and the bad days. The best time to buy salt is before the snowstorm. The best time to buy an umbrella is when it isn't raining. The best time to create plans to overcome challenges in your business is before they happen.

Take a moment and write down the top 10 challenges you face in your daily business. Now write ten potential courses of action for those challenges.

Interesting. The act of writing solutions for those ten challenges will probably reduce those challenges to five because you can likely avoid half of them just by acknowledging they exist.

Delight is being prepared.

#CD365Day170

June 20

"Release obstructions to your natural insight."

–Scott Ginsberg, That Guy with a Nametag

Brian's Take:

Insights, intuition, whatever you want to call it, is the catalyst for your customer "feeling" your true desire to delight them with your product and service.

Take this principle up a notch by making it safe for your employees to use their intuition serving your customers. I assure you, they will stumble onto more success than failure.

Intuition often is the tool that is missing in the traditional customer-service transaction. Give your team an extra tool for their Customer Delight tool box. Your customers won't be sorry.

#CD365Day171

June 21

"Anytime you're tempted to upsell someone else, stop what you're doing and upserve instead."

–Daniel H. Pink

Brian's Take:

There's nothing wrong with the upsell in business. But if you're looking to delight your customer, consider the upserve.

Upserving is a long-term strategy for creating lifelong customers.

#CD365Day172

June 22

"People don't like to be sold—but they love to buy."

–Jeffrey Gitomer

Brian's Take:

Gitomer's 11 words are the difference between being an average company and a great company.

A great company seeks to create products and services that people want. An average company tries to convince you that you need what they have.

When you create great products and services, there's no need to convince. And there's a good chance they will buy!

#CD365Day173

June 23

"Be enthusiastic. Remember the placebo effect—30% of medicine is showbiz."

–Ronald Spark

Brian's Take:

I wonder if "Spark" is his real last name or a stage name. If it's his real name, maybe that's what led him to be an expert on enthusiasm.

Anyway, in customer service, it's not OK to fake the quality of your product, but it's surely OK to fake your enthusiasm. According to Mr. Spark, it might, in fact, actually be a cure for the common grump.

My prescription for creating Customer Delight: two spoons full of sugar and one cup of enthusiasm.

#CD365Day174

June 24

"Sow a thought, reap an action; sow an action, reap a habit; sow a habit, reap a character; sow a character, reap a destiny."

–Stephen Covey

Brian's Take:

What are you sowing in your business to create a legacy of delight?

Let me add to Covey's model: Reap a destiny, sow a legacy, reap a legacy of delight.

#CD365Day175

June 25

"Saying thank you is more than good manners. It is good spirituality."

–Alfred Painter

Brian's Take:

And when it comes to Customer Delight, saying "thank you" is nonnegotiable.

Get 'er done!

#CD365Day176

June 26

"Keep a good attitude and do the right thing even when it's hard. When you do that you are passing the test. And God promises you your marked moments are on their way."

–Joel Osteen

Brian's Take:

True customer delight is often won when times are tough. It's easy to keep a good attitude on a sunny day, but when the storm rolls in, that's an opportunity to create a customer for life.

It's a marked moment with your client. They will remember how you handled the moment.

#CD365Day177

June 27

"Of all the senses, sight must be the most delightful."

–Helen Keller

Brian's Take:

I don't necessarily agree with Helen Keller, but there are some clues in her preference. Delight often stems from lack.

When you can identify a particular lack your client might be experiencing and you can fill it, delight is a certain outcome.

#CD365Day178

June 28

"If you do what you've always done, you'll get what you've always gotten."

–Tony Robbins

Brian's Take:

I'm not sure if Tony Robbins is the originator of this quote or the one who made it famous. What I do know is that if things aren't working for your life and business, it's time to do something different.

The famous definition of insanity, "Doing the same thing over and over, expecting different results," is all too common in failing businesses. Hint: The truth in business is that doing the same thing over and over is generally a recipe for failure.

Humans thrive on variety. What delighted yesterday may not delight on Thursday.

Delight: Keep it fresh!

#CD365Day179

June 29

"A business exists to create a customer."

–Peter F. Drucker

Brian's Take:

Which begs the question, "How do you create a customer?"

Are you shooting arrows in the dark or taking the time to aim and answer the question, "How do I create Customer Delight for my customer?"

Hint: An intentional approach to creating customers is more delightful to the customer than stumbling onto it by accident.

#CD365Day180

June 30

"Build a better mousetrap and the world will beat a path to your door."

–Ralph Waldo Emerson

Brian's Take:

Stop!!!! This is not an opportunity for you to get back to making the transaction part of your business better. The old saying, "It's easier to catch a fly with sugar than vinegar," is the better mousetrap I'm talking about.

Seriously, most business have the product and service-improvement portion of their business down pat. It's the people part of their businesses that needs work.

#CD365Day181

Past, Present and Future Delight:

It's bittersweet to share this story and the lessons I learned from my friend, second father, mentor and sparring partner—the late but ever-present Terry Ramstetter.

Terry was the CEO of Prestige AV & Creative Services in Cincinnati, and I began working for him in 1997. He passed away unexpectedly a few months before I published this book.

Terry was a one-of-a-kind man. He taught me a lot and pissed me off a lot. Like most great teachers, he provided his best lessons by being both a rock and a hard place, but he was also there for my best interest. True to form, his death was both a tragedy and an opportunity for me.

As I wrote Customer Delight 365, I struggled with the fact that I didn't have a specific reference to Terry in my book. He is someone who has greatly impacted my life, but for some reason, I was drawing a blank on how to include him in the book. When I sent my second draft to my editor, she said one of my stories, although nice, didn't exactly pass the test for the book. I thought, "Oh, great! I've been working at this for 18 months and now you want a new story."

But as I mentioned, opportunity came from Terry's death. His passing opened up the floodgates for me. One of the most dynamic men I know, Terry was both demanding and generous. I sat in awe of the inspirations he gave me, and he left me with a lifetime of lessons to draw on.

Here's one of my favorite lessons from Terry on creating Customer Delight.

Prestige AV & Creative Services provides audiovisual and production services for corporate meetings, association conferences and nonprofit galas. The nature of our product puts us in a position to work with many organizations that are hosting meetings and events to make a difference in the world. These organizations often do not have the budget to secure the services we provide. Terry, being the generous man he was, always found a way to allow these organizations to get what they needed to serve their mission, whether it be a nonprofit discount, an in-kind donation or a special "sponsorship" discount. Although it often appeared that we were getting some value in return, the sponsorship was never the goal for him. He just liked to help others with what he had. What he had was an audiovisual company through which he could share his generosity.

One particular nonprofit organization that Prestige worked with had nearly zero budget but had significant needs. This organization did research for rare lung diseases. Their annual conference was a hybrid of patients and doctors coming together to move closer to cures for these debilitating diseases. Our discount for this group was always significant. It often was on the level of 75 percent off.

This group, being true stewards of their money, brought their own equipment to events to keep their audiovisual budget to an absolute minimum. Although great from a donor perspective, this created significant challenges for us as a company. The organization continually revised their room assignments to minimize the use of our product. If they could switch a presentation at the last minute to a room that already had audio visual, to avoid an equipment rental, they would do that.

This meant that our highly discounted event was actually the hardest for our company to service. Continual schedule changes meant we wouldn't be able to set our equipment in advance. An additional challenge was that much of the conference was run by dedicated and passionate volunteers who already had many duties on their plate.

This led to a major snafu. During the day, the organization used the hotel's signature ballroom for education sessions; in the evening, they used it for a gala-type dinner. When the education session finished in the midafternoon, one of our staff members removed a projector used during the session, noting it was not on his schedule for use during the gala. Except he was reviewing an old schedule, which to his defense, might have been printed off at lunchtime. It's very uncommon for our company to have that level of schedule change for an event in progress. To add further salt to the situation, he asked a volunteer if the equipment definitely wasn't needed for the evening. She confirmed, and he removed the equipment.

Of course, you know where this is headed. They did need the projector, and no one noticed the projector was missing until the executive director introduced the keynote speaker, who wanted to connect her laptop. Of course, there were many opportunities for all parties to notice this omission prior to this point in the event, but in review, the organization had sent an agenda update including the request for the equipment. So it could be said that Prestige messed up.

After some shuffling, we took care of the situation, but egg was on many of our faces.

The group's board, which was very much insulated from the understanding of the level of donation Prestige gives to this event annually, demanded the group's executive director request a further discount from us. As the account representative for the project, I felt especially frustrated. Errors happen, and by the way, did your board realize we were donating nearly $10,000 in services? I was thinking, "How about a 'thank you'?!" If we were to give any further discount, we might as well be giving them money to service the event for them.

I spoke with Terry, our CEO, about the situation and mentioned that the organization's board president wanted to meet with him. He said he wanted me to handle it. I asked Terry for his stance on the matter, and he said to acknowledge the challenge and hold firm to our project quote. I don't like conflict, so this stressed me out a bit, but my ego wanted to hold the line.

I met with the president of the board and acknowledged her frustrations. She wasn't satisfied with our stance. She wasn't satisfied with our discount (donation). To be honest, I left the meeting pretty angry. She reached out to me again, requesting a meeting with our CEO (Terry). I denied her request based on my previous discussions with Terry. I shared with him where we stood, and he said, have her call me.

In the coming weeks, I saw the president of this organization arrive at our offices for her meeting with Terry. I was expecting he was going to toe the line he asked me to toe.

Later that day, I ran into Terry in the lunchroom. I asked about the meeting. He said that he went ahead and gave her an additional discount, which was higher than what she requested. I was livid. I was thinking to myself, "These jokesters are taking advantage of us, my boss is making me have uncomfortable meetings, and now he is going to jump in and be the hero, giving away the farm."

I blurted out, "I could've done that. Why did you cause me so much pain and waste so much of my time?"

Terry added to his story. He said he had planned to toe the line, but when speaking with the woman, he remembered a relative who had a rare lung disease and suffered. He decided he wanted to be part of the solution. Not only was he giving the organization a rebate for this year, but he also raised our discount in the following year so the organization wouldn't have to bring its own equipment. We would service the event in full.

I have to admit; it took me years to understand the whole of this story.

I'm not sure what you'll see in this story, but here's my take. I think Terry knew we would bend, but he also knew that I needed to experience working with a board president in a difficult situation. He allowed me to experience the pain of dealing with a difficult situation by allowing me to think for myself, speak for myself. He then showed me another way.

I will never forget the beauty of the last part of the story. Terry gave more the next year. He took something from the past—a less-than-desirable situation—and something from the present—a lesson for an employee—and found a solution that moved us all together into the future. I don't see a better outcome for a challenging situation. The customer gets their needs met, and we continue our relationship.

You see, Terry was invested in the delight of the customer (and even more). When you invest in something, you don't throw it out when a challenge presents itself. You protect it.

Key Takeaway: I have a motto I developed after 20 years in the audiovisual business. Technology will fail, people will fail, but we always have the option to resolve and delight. Terry taught me the latter.

July

July 1

"The things you do for yourself are gone when you are gone, but the things you do for others remain as your legacy."

–Kalu Ndukwe Kalu

Brian's Take:

This pretty much sums up the difference between customer satisfaction and Customer Delight.

A satisfied customer will shop around. A delighted customer becomes part of your business's legacy.

#CD365Day182

July 2

"It's great to be great, but its greater to be human."

–Will Rogers

Brian's Take:

This might be one of the simplest ways to create Customer Delight. Put down your professional persona from time to time and just be human. You'll be surprised how people respond when you show up real and human.

Delight is a human experience.

#CD365Day183

July 3

"Confidence is born in your mind & developed by your thoughts and actions. Therefore you are the author of your confidence."

–R.E. Shockley

Brian's Take:

Confidence is an important asset for creating Customer Delight. Confidence is about doing your homework, getting in your practice and knowing your business.

Confidence, therefore, is not so much an outcome but a prerequisite for creating customer delight. Confidence creates delight.

#CD365Day184

July 4

"Stop wasting your time following up with people who never, ever call you back. If they wanted you, they would have hired you already."

–Scott Ginsberg, That Guy with a Nametag

Brian's Take:

We can't be something to everybody. Sometimes the best model is to focus on the bird in hand vs. the two in the bush.

Hint: Your bird in hand is probably friends with the birds in the bush. Serve your bird well, and the other birds of the feather will eventually get together.

#CD365Day185

July 5

"Ninety-nine percent commitment is a bitch. One hundred percent commitment is a cinch."

–Jim Quinn

Brian's Take:

Jim Quinn could easily be the most important person I ever met. Jim developed an experiential personal-development seminar called Basic. For me, the Basic Seminar was a journey where I was able to get my answers questioned.

One of the mantras from the Basic Seminar was around the concept of commitment. Ninety-nine percent commitment is akin to failure. Anything less than 100 percent commitment isn't worth it.

Often, the difference between customer satisfaction and Customer Delight is a mere one percent, but the difference in outcome is as wide as the Grand Canyon.

#CD365Day186

July 6

"A man without a smiling face must not open a shop."

–Chinese proverb

Brian's Take:

Duh! Have a nice day ☺ is the way to go. A smile is not only contagious, but it also reduces stress. Another positive of smiling is it costs nothing extra, but it drives revenue.

I'm for that. How about you?

#CD365Day187

July 7

"The smallest act of kindness is worth more than the grandest intention."

–Oscar Wilde

Brian's Take:

Most companies have great ideas about how to create a great customer experience, but great companies implement their great ideas.

#CD365Day188

July 8

"You know you are on the road to success if you would do your job, and not be paid for it."

–Oprah Winfrey

Brian's Take:

Some of the best successes in life are stumbled upon through passion, instead of focusing on a mere financial reward. I've noticed that the most successful businesses are run by people who have a passion for their work first and the financial reward is secondary.

When you're pondering a career in customer service, consider if you'll be able to find delight in your work, even if a financial reward isn't present.

#CD365Day189

July 9

"Empathy is about standing in someone else's shoes, feeling with his or her heart, seeing with his or her eyes. Not only is empathy hard to outsource and automate, but it makes the world a better place."

–Daniel H. Pink

Brian's Take:

Customer Delight is hard to outsource.

I recommend first hiring people with delight already in their hearts. Allow them to make your customer's world a better place, which creates more delighted people in the world...who are now good candidates for you to hire.

#CD365Day190

July 10

"Do one thing every day that scares you."

–Eleanor Roosevelt

Brian's Take:

Great customer service requires a zest for life. Brushing up against what scares us is a great way to expand your perspective and unleash your zest. The wider your perspective, the greater your ability to connect with more people.

Eyes wide open!

#CD365Day191

July 11

"Implement a pricing strategy that would make the competition want to come to your office and choke you."

–Scott Ginsberg, That Guy with a Nametag

Brian's Take:

You know you're onto something when your competition stops and takes notice. Why would your competition stop and take notice? Because you've created a reason for your customers to notice—a reason that's noteworthy, different and value-oriented.

I'm a longtime follower of Scott Ginsberg, and I think he needs to provide boxing lessons with his customer-service training because if you follow his ideas, you'll need to defend yourself from the angry competition.

#CD365Day192

July 12

"The single most important thing is to make people happy. If you are making people happy, as a side effect, they will be happy to open up their wallets and pay you."

–Derek Sivers

Brian's Take:

Not that it's about the money, but it is about the money.

Creating happy and delighted customers is a self-fulfilling prophecy. Happy customers mean more money, meaning more happiness for you, meaning more happiness to share with customers, meaning more money...

#CD365Day193

July 13

"It's better to hang out with people better than you. Pick out associates whose behavior is better than yours and you'll drift in that direction."

–Warren Buffett

Brian's Take:

If Warren Buffett is giving advice, I recommend you take it. You could say he is the E.F. Hutton of our generation—when Warren talks, we listen.

I've heard that we are the sum of the five people we spend the most time with. Does the sum of your top five relationships add up to a great customer experience?

#CD365Day194

July 14

"You must be the change you wish to see in the world."

–Mahatma Gandhi

Brian's Take:

It appears this quote might be the answer to all of life's challenges, which includes creating loyal customers.

Hint: Be delightful.

#CD365Day195

July 15

"Take things as they are. Punch when you have to punch. Kick when you have to kick."

–Bruce Lee

Brian's Take:

I'm not sure if this is what Bruce Lee is talking about, but have you ever had a really bad interaction with a company representative where they bite your head off for no reason?

When that happens, I suspect it's because they're taking things as they were. They had a bad morning, they spilled their coffee, or they missed the bus. All things in the past.

As customer-service professionals, we must have strategies for leaving the past behind. Delight is about meeting our customers in the moment, where they are, with what they need in the moment.

If you have a bag of the past slung over your shoulder, when the present shows up, it's hard to lift up delight for your customers.

#CD365Day196

July 16

"When you enchant people, your goal is not to make money from them or to get them to do what you want, but to fill them with great delight."

–Guy Kawasaki

Brian's Take:

Customer service is a chance to take your customers on an enchanted voyage. Enchanting your customers requires you to engage all the senses. How have you created your customer-service experience to engage multiple senses?

Sight, sound, smell, taste and touch. When connected, these senses enchant the heart with delight.

#CD365Day197

July 17

"The key is to set realistic customer expectations, and then not to just meet them, but to exceed them—preferably in unexpected and helpful ways."

–Sir Richard Branson

Brian's Take:

Surprise your customers—in a good way—and you are well on your way to creating extreme customer delight.

At a favorite restaurant of mine, the manager periodically gives me a free cookie, drink or chips. It's not based on any formal rewards program, just a simple surprise that always leaves me smiling.

#CD365Day198

July 18

"Well, you know, I was a human being before I became a businessman."

–George Soros

Brian's Take:

Same with your customers!

#CD365Day199

July 19

"We are not prospecting. We are meeting future customers."

–Tony Ramstetter

Brian's Take:

Prestige AV & Creative Services, my longtime employer, has taught me many lessons about creating delight for customers.

One of the benefits of working for a small organization is that you get to work directly with the company founders. Founders are a special breed of business owner. They often just have that "it" factor.

After nearly two decades of working with Tony (who co-owned the company with his brother, Terry), I can say my customer-service lessons are boundless. While writing this book, I mentioned to Tony that I was traveling to an industry conference to meet prospective customers. He corrected me and called them "future customers."

Small shift in words, major shift in delight as I thought about the customers I would meet.

#CD365Day200

July 20

"Words are plentiful; deeds are precious."

–Lech Walesa

Brian's Take:

A related take on this concept is the title of a book by Pete Blackshaw: *Satisfied Customers Tell Three Friends, Angry Customers Tell 3,000.* So, yes, deeds are precious and words are plentiful.

What kind of deeds will you provide your customers?

I haven't reached out to Pete about how many people delighted customers tell, but I'm sure it's somewhere between three and 3000.

#CD365Day201

July 21

"Profit in business comes from repeat customers; customers that boast about your product and service, and that bring friends with them."

–W. Edwards Deming

Brian's Take:

What is it about our product or service that is going to delight your customer enough for them to invite their friends along for the ride?

Customer Delight is code for making friends—and profit.

#CD365Day202

July 22

"Don't worry, be crappy. Revolutionary means you ship and then test... Lots of things made the first Mac in 1984 a piece of crap—but it was a revolutionary piece of crap."

–Guy Kawasaki

Brian's Take:

This is not a Monopoly "Get Out of Jail Free" card to start serving up crap. But it is an anthem for innovation and revolution.

Innovation is a sibling of delight. Don't worry, delight!

#CD365Day203

July 23

"A cloudy day is no match for a sunny disposition."

–William Arthur Ward

Brian's Take:

Are you a cloud or the sun for your customers? Clouds block de-light.

What is the weathercast for your organization? Are your employees partly cloudy with a chance of showers or clear skies with a chance of delight?

#CD365Day204

July 24

"If you're going through hell, keep going."

–Winston Churchill

Brian's Take:

A bad customer experience might seem like an opportunity to let your guard down, but studies show that if you can weather the storm by acknowledging and resolving a customer-service challenge, your customer's loyalty will go up infinitely.

If you consider challenges to be opportunities, you'll be amazed at the delightful outcome of making things good.

Keep your head up and your eye on the prize!

#CD365Day205

July 25

"The best portion of a good man's life: His little, nameless unremembered acts of kindness and love."

–William Wordsworth

Brian's Take:

Some of your best work as a customer-service professional will never be acknowledged. That's no excuse for not seeking delight.

It's better to have delighted without acknowledgment than to have never delighted at all.

#CD365Day206

July 26

"I don't pay good wages because I have a lot of money; I have a lot of money because I pay good wages."

–Robert Bosch

Brian's Take:

How much are you paying your frontline employees? It makes a difference.

Pay for delight. That is what your customers are paying for when they pay you.

#CD365Day207

July 27

"Courteous treatment will make a customer a walking advertisement."

–James Cash Penney

Brian's Take:

Why pay for advertising when being courteous is a free way to gain advertising?

#CD365Day208

July 28

"We are what we repeatedly do. Excellence, therefore, is not an act but a habit."

–Aristotle

Brian's Take:

The habit of excellence is also a precursor for delight.

Rinse, repeat, delight!

#CD365Day209

July 29

"Give thanks for a little and you will find a lot."

–Hausa Proverb

Brian's Take:

It's been said that you reap what you sow, but it appears we can actually reap more by giving thanks, according to this Hausa proverb. I don't know if there's any data to back this up, but I would say it can't hurt.

I'm thankful for the delight your customers will find in your gratitude.

#CD365Day210

July 30

"Make a customer, not a sale."

–Katherine Barchetti

Brian's Take:

Many companies spend a vast amount of energy focused on creating a business plan, which leads to a company that can become more focused on the "sale" versus the customer.

A recipe for business success is often as simple as shifting your focus from making a sale to making the customer feel good. Feeling good is also known as delight.

#CD365Day211

July 31

"Success is not counted by how high you have climbed but by how many people you brought with you."

–Dr. Wil Rose

Brian's Take:

There's really no glory in going it alone. Humans are relational.

If your vision for business success doesn't include others, you really have no vision for success.

Who is on your journey to the summit? I recommend you include your family, employees, coworkers and customers, because delight in solitude is really just a desert mirage with no substance.

#CD365Day212

August

August 1

"Waiting for perfect is never as smart as making progress."

–Seth Godin

Brian's Take:

Delight is not a destination but a journey. If, by chance, you ever do find perfect delight for your customers, the formula will change.

With Godin's mantra of making progress over perfection, you can create continuous momentum in the direction of delight for your customers. An object at rest tends to stay at rest. An object in motion tends to delight.

#CD365Day213

August 2

"In fact, researchers have settled on what they believe is the magic number for true expertise: ten thousand hours."

–Malcom Gladwell

Brian's Take:

I'm not sure if we can ever confirm that 10,000 hours of practice or experience is the magic number, but I can assure you that it won't hurt.

My recommendation is that you intentionally seek to train your employees with a specific number of hours of practice and experience in order to create expertise in Customer Delight.

Hint: Reading this book takes about three hours. You only have 9,997 to go.

#CD365Day214

August 3

"'Enrapture' is one of the synonyms listed for the word 'delight.' I looked up the word 'enrapture' and one of its definitions is 'to delight beyond measure.' Now that seems like a worthy goal."

–Brian Monahan

Brian's Take:

I guess I have the title for my next book: *Client Enrapture 365: Beyond Measure!*

#CD365Day215

August 4

"Customers long to interact with—even relate to—employees who act like there is still a light on inside."

–Chip Bell

Brian's Take:

It's a sad state of affairs if customer expectations are for nothing more than a warm body. This is actually a great opportunity for those of us who are in customer service to stand out from the competition.

When it comes to Customer Delight, I recommend skipping the mood lighting, and instead, running your employees at full intensity.

#CD365Day216

August 5

"Relationships lead to success. No matter how technical the world gets, opportunities happen through people."

–Emily Thomas

Brian's Take:

Customer Delight is about building a relationship with our customer. If you are in what seems to be a transaction business, you might think that a relationship isn't a factor in your success.

For me, the word "relationship" often conjures thoughts of tenure or length; most good relationships have history, but it's not a prerequisite for a relationship.

The root of "relationship" is simply "relate." I recommend those in transactional businesses consider how you relate to your ideal customer. Then relate with your new mythical ideal customer every time someone new enters your business.

You now have the tenure and history that I mentioned.

#CD365Day217

August 6

"Customer Satisfaction is Worthless, Customer Loyalty is Priceless."

–Jeffrey Gitomer

Brian's Take:

Loyalty is a byproduct of Customer Delight. When you bring together all the elements of Customer Delight into one package, you win the ultimate prize in business: customer loyalty.

Customer loyalty is kind of like an interest-bearing account. The longer you invest in your client (account), the greater your investment begins to pay returns (loyalty).

What's really cool about loyalty is that it actually transcends Customer Delight, allowing for the occasional misstep.

Rule #1 about loyalty: Never count on it. Instead, invest in it.

Read those last two sentences again!

#CD365Day218

August 7

"Perpetual optimism is a force multiplier."

–Colin Powell

Brian's Take:

Would you rather add or multiply your business?

I choose the latter. Optimism pays the bills in business. Delight!

#CD365Day219

August 8

"I can't understand why people are frightened of new ideas. I'm frightened of the old ones."

–John Cage

Brian's Take:

Creating Customer Delight is closely tied to innovation, surprise and new ideas. If you want to delight your customers, you'll eventually need to release some old ideas and values.

Idea! Hang up some old habits and see if your customers notice. If they miss them, you can always bring them back with a nostalgic flair.

#CD365Day220

August 9

"Enthusiasm is the mother of effort, and without it nothing great ever achieved."

–Ralph Waldo Emerson

Brian's Take:

The chemical formula for the make-up of Customer Delight would surely include enthusiasm.

#CD365Day221

August 10

"Cheers to a new year and another chance for us to get it right."

–Oprah Winfrey

Brian's Take:

Oprah's cheers are a great way to think about New Year's Resolutions, but Customer Delight requires a new resolution for every customer in our presence.

A new customer, another chance for you to get it right. All day, every day…Customer Delight!

#CD365Day222

August 11

"Whether you think you can or whether you think you can't, you're right!"

–Henry Ford

Brian's Take:

Be right about delight!

I think you can, I know you can!

#CD365Day223

August 12

"Why wait to be memorable?"

–Tony Robbins

Brian's Take:

For most people, it's safer to maintain the status quo. But in today's business climate, the status quo is a recipe for disaster. Embracing and creating change is the only safe game to play.

Are you playing it safe or creating delight? Get to work!

#CD365Day224

August 13

"Busy does not equal important. Measured doesn't mean mattered."

–Seth Godin

Brian's Take:

Your customers don't care how busy you are. Your customers don't care what your costs are. Your customer simply cares about themselves.

Find the time and the meaning in serving your customer. Delight in the calm of meaningful customer experience.

#CD365Day225

August 14

"A man should never neglect his family for business."

–Walt Disney

Brian's Take:

We must always remember to take care of our own house, or we have no chance to serve delight.

Disney knows a thing or two about delight.

#CD365Day226

August 15

"Difficulties mastered are opportunities won."

–Winston Churchill

Brian's Take:

After working with technology for more than 20 years, I've come to a conclusion: Technology will fail! I've worked in customer service for almost as long, and I've determined that difficulties will happen.

I recommend that you have a plan for difficulties. Delight in your difficulties—they are opportunities in disguise.

#CD365Day227

August 16

"You can't wait for inspiration, you have to go after it with a club."

–Jack London

Brian's Take:

My greatest source of inspiration has almost always included perspiration. Only through the act of solving problems can we get close enough to them to understand them.

To create delight, you must get close to your customers—walking in their shoes, understanding their hearts' desires and challenges. Then you bring meaning to your product and service.

Meaning is the secret weapon of delight. It's the meat in your sandwich. It's the jelly in your donut.

#CD365Day228

August 17

"If you're not serving the customer, you'd better be serving someone who is."

–Karl Albrecht

Brian's Take:

We all have customers; some of them just happen to be on our own team.

Delight in each other and the customer will surely notice.

#CD365Day229

August 18

"When you're trying to make an important decision, and you're sort of divided on the issue, ask yourself: If the customer were here, what would she say?"

–Dharmesh Shah

Brian's Take:

I often use a similar technique when working with an upset customer. I apologize that their customer experience didn't meet expectations. I accept fault for my/our failure. Then I ask the customer what I can do to rectify the situation.

We often think we know what the customer wants but without asking, we're really just guessing.

Ask your customer and manifest delight.

#CD365Day230

August 19

"The best way to cheer yourself up: Cheer everybody else up."

–Mark Twain

Brian's Take:

Twain might have shared one of the biggest secrets of life, but it's not really about cheering people up. It's about taking our focus outward.

A healthy outward focus is a distraction to the "yap, yap" voice in our head that's often looking to bring us down. When you do for others, your brain is "tricked" into seeing a different world. A world that is good. A self-fulfilling reality.

OK, that's a bit deep for a customer-experience book. But isn't that really the problem with customer service these days? Delight isn't shallow. Delight is deep.

#CD365Day231

August 20

"Simplicity is the ultimate sophistication."

–Leonardo da Vinci

Brian's Take:

Are you going to question Da Vinci, one of the greatest minds and artists of all time?

When it comes to customer delight, don't confuse simplicity with lack. Some of the greatest work is the pursuit of simple. For your customer, simple might be a lifetime of experience serving that customer.

What is one thing you can do today to simplify your product or service?

Simply delight!

#CD365Day232

August 21

"The man with a new idea is a crank until the idea succeeds."

–Mark Twain

Brian's Take:

Do you have the courage to be a crank while serving your customers? Sometimes the best ideas are the most unlikely bedfellows.

What ideas are you holding back that could be delighting your customers? Fear is the arch enemy of delight. Step up with courage and be prepared to be the crank. Your customers will find it delightful.

#CD365Day233

August 22

"The trouble with the future is that is usually arrives before we're ready for it."

–Arnold H. Glasow

Brian's Take:

The trouble with most companies is they spend most of their time reacting vs. looking ahead. When we fail to look into the future, we fail the customer.

I predict the companies that look into the future and plan for the future will have the greatest opportunity for delighting their customers.

Delight is created by creating a vision of a future customer connection.

#CD365Day234

August 23

"Principles before Rules. Progress before Perfection."

–Michael Hartzell

Brian's Take:

This might be the simplest formula I have come across for creating excessive Customer Delight. Applying rules over principles is similar to missing the forest for the trees.

We can't plan for all of life's scenarios, but we can have principles and values that guide us when faced with situations that seem to fall outside the lines. Principle-driven business stand out from the competition like a beacon in the dark.

Then, of course, progress before perfection. If you agree that you can't plan for every scenario, you understand that perfection is an unattainable goal that diminishes your ability to connect and create delight.

#CD365Day235

August 24

"Two people can have a middling day, but one rounds up and the other rounds down."

–Robert Brault

Brian's Take:

The difference between despair and delight: a rounding error.

When it comes to delight the rule is simple: Round up!

#CD365Day236

August 25

"To know and not to do is really not to know."

–Stephen Covey

Brian's Take:

I'm not going to be as easy on you as Covey. Consistently ask yourself this question: "Based on what I know up to this point in my life, what would be the best way to proceed?" Then proceed.

I know you know delight. Do it!

#CD365Day237

August 26

"Our life is frittered away by detail...Simplicity, simplicity, simplicity! I say, let our affairs be as two or three, and not a hundred or a thousand...Simplify, simplify!"

–Henry David Thoreau

Brian's Take:

Here are some ways you might simplify your customers buying experience.

- home delivery
- concierge service
- free/automatic refills
- online ordering
- drive through window
- unlimited access
- 24-hour service

Now be the first to offer it in your industry. There was a time when pizza was only available via horseback. Delight is simple and convenient.

#CD365Day238

August 27

"I GET to take out the garbage."

–Mike Monahan

Brian's Take:

Sometimes something as simple as a word exchange can make all the difference in the world. Many would say, "I HAVE to take out the garbage," but not my dear old Dad. He always says, "I GET to take out the garbage. Get out of my way. This is my job. I am taking out the garbage, and I love it!"

How is your approach to your customers? Do you have to serve them or do you get to create delight?

I get to share this book with you! And it's a blast!

#CD365Day239

August 28

"Throwing yourself into a job you enjoy is one of the life's greatest pleasures!"

–Sir Richard Branson

Brian's Take:

This might be the most important factor when it comes to creating Customer Delight. If you fail to find a job that you can throw yourself into, it becomes challenging to find the joy and pleasure.

But if you haven't found the right job, try throwing yourself into what you have. Interestingly, you'll probably find great pleasure.

Give it a try. I'm interested to hear if the great pleasure is more about you or the job. If that doesn't work, throw yourself into creating great pleasure for your customers.

#CD365Day240

August 29

"Gratitude is the memory of the heart."

–Jean Baptiste Massieu

Brian's Take:

One of my favorite discoveries while writing this book was the idea of delight being in the heart of the beholder. This leads to another factor when you desire to create delight for your customers. It's my belief that the language of the heart is only delivered and received by the heart, which means that for you to create it, you must remember it.

Remember your heart and share your delight.

#CD365Day241

August 30

"How was your day?" is a question that matters a lot more than it seems."

–Seth Godin

Brian's Take:

Does your product or service improve the quality of one's day, or is it invisible?

As a business, you always have the opportunity to be part of a person's "How was your day?" story.

Hopefully, your part is delightful.

#CD365Day242

August 31

"No duty is more urgent than that of returning thanks."

–James Allen

Brian's Take:

When it come to Customer Delight, it's not just a good idea to be thankful for your customers—it's your duty.

Get thankful. Duty calls!

#CD365Day243

September

September 1

"You are never too old to set another goal or to dream a new dream."

–C.S. Lewis

Brian's Take:

It's never too late in the day to serve your customer. It's never too late to learn a new technique for excellent customer service. It's never too late to make someone smile. It's never too late until it is too late, and even then you have an opportunity for redemption.

Unless you're six feet under, in my mind, you're obligated to continue to serve your coworkers, your customers and humanity.

#CD365Day244

September 2

"Be the light in the dark, be the calm in the storm and be at peace while at war."

–Mike Dolan

Brian's Take:

The keyword in Dolan's quote is "Be."

Be light, be delight.

#CD365Day245

September 3

"One of the deep secrets of life is that all that is really worth doing is what we do for others."

–Lewis Carroll

Brian's Take:

One of the deep secrets of business is that a career in customer service is one of the greatest works one can do.

The true beauty of a passionate customer-service professional is when he shifts from wanting to serve to an attitude of "getting" to serve.

#CD365Day246

September 4

"Do what you say you are going to do, when you say you are going to do it, in the way you said you were going to do it."

–Larry Winget

Brian's Take:

You've got to meet Larry sometime: He is a no-holds-barred kind of guy. He says it like it is, but he also walks the talk.

The best businesses focus more on keeping their commitments than flashy marketing. Don't let your mouth offer up what your feet can't deliver.

#CD365Day247

September 5

"Making money is art and working is art and good business is the best art."

–Andy Warhol

Brian's Take:

I consider myself much more of an artist than a business professional. What could be more creative than painting a smile on your customer's face?

Have a nice day!

#CD365Day248

September 6

"Always do more than is required of you."

–George S. Patton

Brian's Take:

I've seen so many people fail at this principle. It's like the story of the man who stood in front of his fireplace and said, "I will give you wood, when you give me heat." Of course, he froze to death.

Many businesses are freezing to death with plenty of wood on the hearth. Kindle delight.

#CD365Day249

September 7

"The undisciplined are slaves to moods, appetites and passions."

–Stephen Covey

Brian's Take:

Your business needs to be disciplined in infusing delight in your employees. What is your plan to create smiling, happy employees? Oh, you don't have a plan? Fail to plan for delight, fail to delight.

Idea: Ask every employee in your organization to read from *Customer Delight 365* daily. This takes discipline, but I promise you a common mantra for delight will change your organization and business in ways you can never imagine.

#CD365Day250

September 8

"The soul that perpetually overflows with kindness and sympathy will always be cheerful."

–Parke Godwin

Brian's Take:

What kind of souls are you hiring for your company's front line? I recommend the kind and compassionate, a.k.a. the cheerful and delightful.

#CD365Day251

September 9

"Yesterday's home runs don't win today's games."

–Babe Ruth

Brian's Take:

How are you continually renewing your spirit to provide Customer Delight?

Don't get nostalgic about past customer-delight successes. Customers have short memory spans, so keep the delight fresh and front of mind.

#CD365Day252

September 10

"I want to put a ding in the universe."

–Steve Jobs

Brian's Take:

I want to put delight in the universe. I want to inspire you to put delight in the universe.

#CD365Day253

September 11

"Kind words can be short and easy to speak, but their echoes are truly endless."

–Mother Teresa

Brian's Take:

Unfortunately, the same is true for less than kind words or service.

What kind of echo will you choose for your customers' eternity: disappointment or delight?

#CD365Day254

September 12

"Great things come to those who prepare so when the opportunity comes you have the means to take it."

–R.E. Shockley

Brian's Take:

I'm pretty sure R.E. Shockley's quote sums up the power of Customer Delight. When you prepare to wow your customers with delight, the outcome is often new customers.

Prepared delight is the best plan for business success; however, there's nothing wrong with unexpected delight.

#CD365Day255

September 13

"The next time you're faced with something that's unexpected, unwanted and uncertain, consider that it just may be a gift."

–Stacey Kramer

Brian's Take:

It's easy to get tense when faced with a challenging customer-service scenario, but if you can shift your perspective, challenges become great opportunities.

Numerous studies show that customer loyalty goes up when a company addresses and overcomes a challenge with their clients. Aside from this benefit, you have the choice to view service challenges as an opportunity to grow and learn.

Expect challenges, embrace challenges, and your spirit will be ready to create delight.

#CD365Day256

September 14

"Get closer than ever to your customers. So close, in fact, that you tell them what they need well before they realize it themselves."

–Steve Jobs

Brian's Take:

Some might say Steve Jobs was arrogant and that thinking you know what's best for others is arrogant. That's not what this quote says. It says to get so close to your customers that you know them better than they know themselves.

Anticipation is the underpinning of creating Customer Delight.

#CD365Day257

September 15

"Position yourself well—don't just have clever slogans."

–Scott Ginsberg, That Guy with a Nametag

Brian's Take:

One of my favorite phrases is, "Any result is better than a reason."

Your customers can see right through your slogans. McDonald's says, "I'm loving it." However, if you're not loving it and instead you're hating it...well, that's a problem.

Slogans must be authentic and match the experience. I'm not poo-pooing your inspiration, just make sure your aspirations come with perspiration.

Actions speak louder than words. Actions pay better, too!

#CD365Day258

September 16

"A lot of people have fancy things to say about customer service, but it's just a day-in, day-out, ongoing, never-ending, persevering, compassionate kind of activity."

–Christopher McCormick

Brian's Take:

Alright, Christopher McCormick... Yep, this book has some fancy ideas about Customer Delight—and I'm not going to take them back—but he does have a point.

Unless you're going provide Customer Delight day in and day, out you're setting yourself up for failure. Creating Customer Delight isn't a one time deal, it's as important to a business as the air we breathe.

#CD365Day259

September 17

"People rarely buy what they need. They buy what they want."

–Seth Godin

Brian's Take:

And sometimes people buy just because it makes them feel good.

Put need and delight together, and you have a recipe for success.

#CD365Day260

September 18

"If I really want to improve my situation, I can work on the one thing over which I have control—myself."

–Stephen Covey

Brian's Take:

Don't try to change your customers, change yourself. And that pretty much requires another quote: "Be the change," Mahatma Gandhi said.

I think that if Gandhi and Covey came together and created a customer-service book, it might be called: *Be the Delight!*

#CD365Day261

September 19

"Innovation is creativity with a job to do."

–John Emmerling

Brian's Take:

Ooh la la, I like this one. Where have you been my whole life, John Emmerling?

Early in my career, I created a website called "The Idea Maniac," which was all about compiling creative ideas and solutions to problems. This was a fun idea, but it left a lot to be desired. It didn't have an action component.

Innovation requires action. Nothing wrong with brainstorming, but as I've matured, I've learned that creativity without a job or focus is like a seed for a tree that never gets planted.

I like to think delight is creativity with a customer to serve.

#CD365Day262

September 20

"Have a story. And make sure it's a good one. A DAMN good one."

–Hugh MacLeod

Brian's Take:

Humans are genetically conditioned for stories. Stories have been the method for sharing information since the dawn of civilization.

You're penalizing yourself by not recognizing and sharing the story of you, the story of your business.

By the way, if you can find a way to weave your customers into your storyline in a delightful way, your business will thrive.

#CD365Day263

September 21

"Ever since I was a child I have had this instinctive urge for expansion and growth. To me, the function and duty of a quality human being is the sincere and honest development of one's potential."

–Bruce Lee

Brian's Take:

Creating a world-class customer experience is as simple as hiring Bruce Lee or people like Bruce Lee.

People with an instinctive urge for expansion will always find their way to the high road. Taking the high road in life and in business creates a win-win product, service or experience.

It's much easier to hire employees who have the instinct for growth than to develop it.

#CD365Day264

September 22

"The man who will use his skill and constructive imagination to see how much he can give for a dollar, instead of how little he can give for a dollar, is bound to succeed."

–Henry Ford

Brian's Take:

My goal isn't to get the most from my client but to give them the most for their dollar.

Recommendation: Next time you find yourself head to head with the competition, offer more for the dollar instead of lowering your price. People buy on value, not price.

Always give more for your dollar, and you'll always have a line of customers ready to buy!

#CD365Day265

September 23

"Without a sense of urgency, desire loses its value."

–Jim Rohn

Brian's Take:

This is a fitting quote for my 266th entry for this book. This leaves me with 99 entries to achieve my initial goal of 365 Customer Delight reflections.

With my goal (my sense of urgency) of writing 20 entries per week, I know I can deliver the result of my desires.

Customer service requires a similar urgency. You must have goals, benchmarks and markers to know you're delivering value and delight. If a tree falls in the forest and no one is there to hear it, did a tree really fall?

If you don't document your goals and desires for your client experience, they're kind of like trees falling on deaf ears. Delight is best delivered with intention and urgency.

Customer Delight 365—it's urgent!

#CD365Day266

September 24

"Smile, it's contagious."

–J.D. Meier (on lessons learned from Guy Kawasaki)

Brian's Take:

The best part of sharing a smile is that it doesn't cost a dime. Consider creating a strategy to help your employees smile more. The more they smile, the more your customers smile, the more your bottom line smiles.

Catch a smile.

#CD365Day267

September 25

We've Only Just Begun

–The Carpenters

Brian's Take:

We started this book walking, but it feels like we are running now!

By now, you know I have a corny side. I love my music, my metaphors and my puns. My hope is that as you continue to read *Customer Delight 365*, you hit your own stride for creating Customer Delight.

I hope this book triggers something inside of you. It might be in the area of customer service. It might be a kind word to a stranger. Better yet, it might be a kind word for yourself. Delight is in the heart of the beholder.

Go forth and delight—together!

#CD365Day268

September 26

"Reach for the stars, even if you have to stand on a cactus."

–Susan Longacre

Brian's Take:

I'm pretty sure this describes what it takes to be a successful customer-service professional. Creating delight often comes after the calluses form.

Don't fear the cactus needles? Isn't that a Blue Oyster Cult song? Don't get my joke? Need more cowbell? OK, I will stop.

I got a fever and the only prescription is more delight.

#CD365Day269

September 27

"The human spirit is stronger than anything that can happen to it."

–C.C. Scott

Brian's Take:

Can you imagine carrying this quote into the daily battle called "customer service? Create a little mini-shield and place it on the cash register or on your phone as a fun reminder of just how powerful you really are.

Next time you feel yourself getting anxious that you can't continue to deliver delight, remember that the human spirit is not only stronger but also more delightful than anything that can happen to you.

Delight warriors unite!

#CD365Day270

September 28

"Customer: A person who indirectly pays for all your vacations, hobbies, and golf games and gives you the opportunity to better yourself."

–Unknown

Brian's Take:

Funny, the same could be said for your "boss." Or could "customer" and "boss" be one and the same?

I think this is about perspective. When you see your customers in the right light, it's much easier to stay focused on creating delight.

#CD365Day271

September 29

"Good service is good business."

–Siebel Advertisement

Brian's Take:

This begs the question, "What is delightful service?"
Delightful service is great business.

#CD365Day272

September 30

"That which we persist in doing becomes easier not because the task has changed, but our ability to do it has increased."

–Ralph Waldo Emerson

Brian's Take:

Many careers are derailed when people meet with adversity. Adversity is a liar, trying to sell you the story that it will always be hard. The liar, by far, is the greatest enemy of Customer Delight.

Persist and delight.

#CD365Day273

The Flirty Sandwich Shop

A few years back, a new sandwich shop opened in Cincinnati. It's a fun little shop with an old-time feel, including vintage signs and décor. Plus, they use great ingredients and serve premium sub sandwiches. But the sandwiches and décor are just the beginning of this story.

During my first visits to the sandwich shop, I found myself enjoying their nostalgic atmosphere and tasty subs. At the time, I was in my late thirties—cruising toward the big 4-OH and realizing there was no pill for replacing my MOJO. Those of you on the far side of your thirties (and beyond) probably know what I'm talking about.

But this little sandwich shop seemed to have a secret ingredient to overcome my depleting MOJO: namely, a staff that happened to really dig me. Many of them were young, but they didn't treat me as if I was OLD! They asked me about my day, always ready for a conversation (because, of course, they really dug me).

I became quite the regular, feeding my belly and my ego. As for atmosphere, not only did they like me and have great sandwiches, but they also featured local musicians during lunch and on the weekends. The whole thing made for a vibrant experience.

About a year into my love affair with this sandwich shop, they opened a second location closer to my home. I started to frequent the new store, and lo and behold, this staff dug me, too! I had to chuckle.

I noticed a common theme between the two stores. They had a system: great sandwiches and a chatty staff. No need to hide behind my smartphone, because I had an interested human to connect with. (Did I mention that they dug me?) Sometimes we covered simple topics: *How is your day going? How about the weather lately*? But more often than not, we had conversations about local events, sports, family and plans for the weekend. I wanted to keep believing that it was all about me. But I figured out it was really about their M-O, not just my MOJO.

I told my wife about my little crush on Potbelly Sandwich Shop. I told her the story of how I thought they were really digging me—*just me*—but then realized that it was part of their operating procedures and how their employees are required to engage their customers.

I could've been disappointed. Instead, I became endeared, which is not quite the same as replacing my MOJO. But creating endearment among patrons is a great way to run a company. They're making the world a better place with simple conversation. I suspect not everyone thought the sandwich-makers were flirting with them. But I bet they still walked away feeling a sense of joy at having someone show interest in them.

I think Potbelly is on to something. After all, remember the Dale Carnegie quote we discussed on May 16: "A person's name is to him or her the sweetest and most important sound in any language." In my opinion, the next sweetest sound is hearing yourself talk about yourself.

In a related note, Joni, the manager at my new "home" Potbelly, the one who "crushed" me with her kindness, is one of the best restaurant managers in the business. I consider her part of my #CD365AllStar. She never ceases to amaze me with her customer-service expertise, including random free cookies, discounts when I joke I should get a price break, a free sandwich when I forget my wallet, and genuine interest in my family. Of course, I'm a great customer: I come in three or four times a week, and usually one or two of those visits include my family or co-workers. In fact, I think I might be responsible for introducing at least 25 percent of Joni's customers to this Potbelly location—all of whom are regulars now. Maybe that's exaggerated a bit, but enough about me. (See, I told you that people love to talk about themselves!)

Anyway, Joni is awesome—not only with me, but with all of her customers. She also is great with her employees. If you're ever in Cincinnati, check out The Potbelly Sandwich Shop at Rookwood Commons and be sure to tell Joni that Brian sent you.

Key Takeaway: If you own a business or manage customer-service employees, what kind of policies and procedures do you have in place to touch your customers' hearts or to perk up their MOJO?

October

October 1

"The entrepreneur always searches for change, responds to it, and exploits it as an opportunity."

–Peter Drucker

Brian's Take:

When we seek the opportunity to create delight, exploiting your customer's heart and pocketbook might actually be in his best interest.

#CD365Day274

October 2

"Imagination is everything. It is the preview of life's coming attractions."

-Albert Einstein

Brian's Take:

Imagine everyone enjoys your product or service. Imagine what your next step is to create a delightful customer experience.

Imagine you taking action. Now take it!

#CD365Day275

October 3

"Achievement is talent plus preparation."

–Malcom Gladwell

Brian's Take:

Preparation is a catalyst for delight. When we, as businesses, organizations or service professionals, can prepare and anticipate our customers' needs, challenges and desires, delight is all but guaranteed.

Take a moment to write down your customers' 10 most compelling challenges and prepare a solution to delight.

#CD365Day276

October 4

"The golden rule for every business man is this: 'Put yourself in your customer's place.'"

–Orison Swett Marden

Brian's Take:

I think Marden is asking us to do more than think like our clients. He's asking us to take on their emotions as our customers.

Delight is an emotion.

#CD365Day277

October 5

"There's no shortage of remarkable ideas, what's missing is the will to execute them."

–Seth Godin

Brian's Take:

There's also no shortage of opportunities to delight. What is missing is the will to execute on them.

#CD365Day278

October 6

"We have entered the era of the customer. Today, providing customers with outstanding customer service is essential to building loyal customers and a long lasting brand."

–Jerry Gregoire

Brian's Take:

What is an "era," anyway? It's a period of common belief or interest. Eras don't need to be worldly eras; they can also be applied to smaller groups of individuals.

What era are your customers experiencing? I have a feeling that after reading this book, a lot more companies will enter the Customer Delight Era.

#CD365Day279

October 7

"I attract a crowd, not because I'm an extrovert or I'm over the top or I'm oozing with charisma. It's because I care."

–Gary Vaynerchuk

Brian's Take:

My father was a tradesman for most of his career. Later in his life, he became a seminar facilitator and executive director of a nonprofit organization that teaches people how to find success in life and business.

His education level isn't much more than high school, and he failed the third grade. When he started his second career, his speaking skills were average. But he still was able to create a loyal following because he cared for those he taught. He is now quite the accomplished speaker, but just like Vaynerchuk, his success is about the caring.

Some of my favorite businesses aren't the best at what they sell, but they are the best at caring.

#CD365Day280

October 8

"Make your product easier to buy than your competition, or you will find your customers buying from them, not you."

–Mark Cuban

Brian's Take:

Do you make it easy for your customers to buy? Amazon has had huge success with 1-Click purchasing.

What have you done to make it easier for your customers to buy from you?

#CD365Day281

October 9

"The price of greatness is responsibility."

–Winston Churchill

Brian's Take:

Have you ever stopped to consider the cost of delight? I suspect the price of delight includes responsibility, but it also includes care, humor and humility, to name a few.

Take the time to identify what it takes to deliver delight and create a plan to bring it to life.

#CD365Day282

October 10

"If you're not approachable, your employees will seek answers elsewhere."

–Scott Ginsberg, That Guy with a Nametag

Brian's Take:

The real pain in this quote is that not only will your employees seek answers elsewhere, your customers will too.

It's the circle of delight: approachable manager, approachable employee, delighted customer.

What's the status of your circle of delight?

#CD365Day283

October 11

"You can't stop the waves, but you can learn how to surf."

¬Jon Kabat-Zinn

Brian's Take:

I have a similar take on life as Jon Kabat-Zinn does. After a long day at work, my wife often asks me, "How was your day?" And I often reply with, "I've been dancing since my feet hit the floor this morning."

I believe that creating Customer Delight is about harnessing the daily challenges. You can stand still and let the wave hit you broadside, or you can get on top of it by getting in touch with your enthusiasm and creativity.

If you go with my analogy, creating Customer Delight is like a tango. Someone has to take the lead in the dance.

#CD365Day284

October 12

"Awesomesauce"

–Urban Dictionary

Brian's Take:

I first heard this delightful term on a credit-card commercial. Since then, I can do nothing but smile when I think or say "awesomesauce."

Sly O.D., a commenter on UrbanDictionary.com, defined "awesomesauce" in this way:

"Something that is more awesome than awesome. It is a modifier of your basic awesome into a more awesome version."

Throughout this book, I take a few stabs at a formula or an equation for delight.

I think I have finally stumbled onto something that makes sense. The square root of awesomesauce is Customer Delight 365.

Customer Delight 365^2 = Awesomesauce

#CD365Day285

October 13

"We see our customers as invited guests to a party, and we are the hosts. It's our job to make the customer experience a little bit better."

–Jeff Bezos

Brian's Take:

It's very powerful to create a point of view from which you are serving your client.

I love the idea of "hosting" a party. A good party host creates a place for people to feel welcome and to connect.

Take a moment and ask what point of view you're currently serving your customers. You might be surprised with your point of view.

Would you enjoy your party?

#CD365Day286

October 14

"Treat your customer, as you want to be treated as a customer."

–Catherine Pulsifier

Brian's Take:

If there were 10 Commandments of Customer Delight, this would be one of them. I'm sure its roots are in the Golden Rule: "Do unto others as you would have done to you."

#CD365Day287

October 15

"If you are going to achieve excellence in big things, you develop the habit in little matters. Excellence is not an exception, it is a prevailing attitude."

–Colin Powell

Brian's Take:

Little matters are the biggest matters when it comes to creating Customer Delight. I've dined at the finest of restaurants and left dissatisfied because the table rocks, or the phone ringing at the host stand is annoying, or— even worse—the rest room lacks paper products. None of these issues reduced the quality of the food, but they definitely reduced the quality of my experience.

Remember the small things, and the big things will fall in place.

#CD365Day288

October 16

"Be kind, for everyone you meet is fighting a hard battle."

–Ian MacLaren

Brian's Take:

I think it's easy to dismiss our customers, not because we don't care, but because we get into ruts. If we aren't awake to our customers, they can become transactions.

We all have challenges, which means our customers do, too. You may never know how you make a difference in someone's life, but if you start to give your customers the benefit of the doubt by providing them the delight they deserve, you'll change lives. Sometimes, you might even hear about it. Sometimes, you might get a gushing, "Thank you!"

Trust and be kind.

#CD365Day289

October 17

"You don't take a photograph, you make it."

–Ansel Adams

Brian's Take:

You don't serve your customer, you earn your customer. Not exactly the same as what Ansel Adams is saying, but it's not far off.

I think what Adams is asking us to do is to connect with our creative spirit. When we're connected with our own spirit, it's easier to connect with our client's spirit. That's a much bigger game to play.

Get connected. Make delight.

#CD365Day290

October 18

"A rose on time is more valuable than a $1,000 gift that's too late."

–Jim Rohn

Brian's Take:

It's a shame, but often the simplest way to stand out from the competition is by keeping your word.

In case you don't know it, being on time is the same as keeping your word. Being late is the easiest way to create distrust in a relationship.

Time to buy a watch from a timely jeweler!

#CD365Day291

October 19

"There's a way to do it better—find it."

–Thomas Edison

Brian's Take:

You can accept life as it is, or you can improve on it.

If you are the kind of person who accepts life as it is, you might want to find a job that doesn't include customers. If you can find that job, let me know.

Otherwise, join us in this wonderful journey of seeking and creating delight. It's really the only game in town.

#CD365Day292

October 20

"A complaint is a unique opportunity to strengthen the relationship with the client."

–Kevin Kelly

Brian's Take:

Say what? Yes, a complaint is an opportunity that often leads to a more loyal client—if you can respond and rectify the situation.

Hint: Defending your position isn't a recipe for strengthening a client relationship—it's a detractor.

In complaints, we delight!

#CD365Day293

October 21

"The greatest of all abilities is the power to inspire confidence."

–Napoleon Hill

Brian's Take:

No matter how great your business model, you'll always have transactions that fail. When you empower your frontline employees with the ability to handle customer challenges on the spot, it instills (inspires) confidence in your customers that you have their best interests at heart.

Notice we're instilling confidence not just in our employees but also in our customers.

Win-Win, Delight-Delight!

#CD365Day294

October 22

"My friends, love is better than anger. Hope is better than fear. Optimism is better than despair. So let us be loving, hopeful and optimistic. And we'll change the world."

–Jack Layton

Brian's Take:

My friends, the moral of this story is, "Delight is better than satisfaction." It's just like the title of the immortal Rolling Stones' song, *(I Can't Get No) Satisfaction.*

Satisfaction is an elusive and low target. Delight is a higher calling. Delight can change the world.

P.S. I felt funny early in this book when I equated Customer Delight with being a world-changing mission, but after discovering Layton's quote, I think we're onto something. Our world is delightful!

#CD365Day295

October 23

"What you do makes a difference, and you have to decide what kind of difference you want to make."

–Jane Goodall

Brian's Take:

Customer Delight is a conscious act of conscious service, which means you must decide to deliver a great customer experience.

Are you going through the motions with your customers?

#CD365Day296

October 24

"Change is not merely necessary to life—it is life."

–Alvin Toffler

Brian's Take:

If you're not preparing yourself or your employees for change, you're not preparing your customers for delight.

Change is a constant, delight is a byproduct. Change isn't a reason for lack of delight, it is a base for delight.

You are the catalyst. Cataclysmic delight. Wowee-kowee!

#CD365Day297

October 25

"If you're competitor-focused, you have to wait until there is a competitor doing something. Being customer-focused allows you to be more pioneering."

–Jeff Bezos

Brian's Take:

Have you taken the time to analyze your customers? Customer focus requires a blend of listening, anticipating and innovating—a direct catalyst for creating an environment of Customer Delight.

#CD365Day298

October 26

"Make a mantra, not a mission."

–Guy Kawasaki

Brian's Take:

Guy Kawasaki goes on to say that a mission statement is often too big to be effective in today's fast-paced business climate. We need something short and sweet.

I also believe that a mantra has an element of action, where a mission seems to be more of a statement. I equate a mantra as a state of being and a mission as a state of telling.

No tell delight. Be delight.

#CD365Day299

October 27

"Sometimes we are limited more by attitude than by opportunities."

–Anonymous

Brian's Take:

This is an interesting quote because it equates attitude and opportunities. I actually see attitude as a catalyst for opportunities.

Opportunity rarely shows up as a gift, wrapped with a bow. Instead, opportunities are self-fulfilling gifts. When you take something challenging or bad and clean it up, spruce it up and wrap it up with your positive attitude, you create the gift of opportunity for yourself and your customers.

Delight is a self-fulfilling prophecy.

#CD365Day300

October 28

"To be a great champion you must believe you are the best. If you're not, pretend you are."

–Muhammad Ali

Brian's Take:

"Float like a butterfly, sting like a bee," wasn't a silly phrase for Ali. He pretended this mantra was true, and it became true.

It's kind of like the eternal question of what came first—the chicken or the egg. Except there's no mystery when it comes to Ali: I'm sure pretending came first.

Pretend to delight your customers daily!

#CD365Day301

October 29

"A thousand words will not leave so deep an impression as one deed."

–Henrik Ibsen

Brian's Take:

Save your breath. Actions speak louder than words and marketing.

Marketing is like giving yourself a nickname. You can't give yourself a nickname—only the people who love you can give you a nickname.

What nickname will your customers give you for your deeds?

#CD365Day302

October 30

"Live with passion."

–Tony Robbins

Brian's Take:

So many people confuse the word "passion" with "joy." "Passion" actually has its roots in "pain," which is an almost unbearable or controllable emotion.

I think it's important to understand that not every day will feel joyful when you work in customer service. It requires a counterintuitive desire to overcome challenge and pain with a vision for the summit.

The summit is often the shortest part of the journey, which means we need passion for the longest part of the journey.

Delight in the journey. Delight in the summit. Delight for your customers!

#CD365Day303

October 31

"There is a spiritual aspect to our lives—when we give, we receive—when a business does something good for somebody, that somebody feels good about them!"

–Ben Cohen

Brian's Take:

I don't think it's by accident that we refer to the "mind, body and spirit." We could say, "spirit, mind and body," but most of us just don't flow that way.

Customer service often ends at mind and body, but when we find a way to connect with spirit, it's a whole new game. Who'da thunk that your customers might actually feel good about you?

Delight in the spirit of doing good for others.

#CD365Day304

November

November 1

"To think creatively, we must be able to look afresh at what we normally take for granted."

–George Kneller

Brian's Take:

Customer Delight is created by adding creativity to the process of customer service.

A great technique for creating Customer Delight is to imagine yourself as the customer of your business. How does it feel?

#CD365Day305

November 2

"Admission of ignorance is often the first step in our education."

–Stephen Covey

Brian's Take:

This might be one of the most powerful concepts in customer service that you'll ever read. It's easy to deliver great customer service when everything is going well. It's when we screw up that things start to fall apart. This is where great organizations flat out destroy average organizations.

Have a plan and process for responding to challenges. First, acknowledge the problem. Then accept responsibility for the challenge. Now listen to the customer and learn.

Challenges are an education for creating future delight.

#CD365Day306

November 3

"Assemble your purpose. Make it your map. Then validate your existence on a daily basis."

–Scott Ginsberg, That Guy with a Nametag

Brian's Take:

I don't really have much to add to this. If you take this prescription daily and share it with your employees, you can't miss.

Delight begins at home. Take care of your soul and your customers will validate and delight—on purpose!

#CD365Day307

November 4

"Successful people are always looking for opportunities to help others. Unsuccessful people are always asking, 'What's in it for me?'"

–Brian Tracy

Brian's Take:

If you're listening to WIIFM (What's In It For Me?) Radio and you're a customer-service professional, you've tuned into the wrong station. WIIFM is for customers.

Your station is KSAS (Keep Smiling And Serving). You can pick up KSAS worldwide; you just need to remember to tune in.

#CD365Day308

November 5

"Go beyond merely communicating to 'connecting' with people."

—Jerry Bruckner

Brian's Take:

The world has gone through all kinds of stages from the Paleozoic to the Industrial Revolution to the Information Age.

I believe we're in the Connecting Age, where the opportunity to connect in a meaningful way has expanded exponentially. Isolated, closed and directional communication are no longer acceptable.

Connecting requires more energy from you, but the payoff is worth the price.

#CD365Day309

November 6

"Remember not only to say the right thing in the right place, but far more difficult still, to leave unsaid the wrong thing at the tempting moment."

–Benjamin Franklin

Brian's Take:

Customer Delight sometimes involves a calloused tongue. Bite down for delight!

#CD365Day310

347

November 7

"The NBA is never just a business. It's always business. It's always personal. All good businesses are personal. The best businesses are very personal."

–Mark Cuban

Brian's Take:

Get personal. Give delight.

November 8

"Sell practical, tested merchandise at reasonable profit, treat your customers like human beings—and they will always come back."

–L.L. Bean

Brian's Take:

What does it really mean to treat your customers like "human beings," anyway? I think it's a shift from looking at your customer as a transaction to seeing them as your brother, mother, your family. What would you do for your family with no expectation in return?

When you can do the same for your customers as you would do for your family, they will notice the difference.

#CD365Day312

November 9

"An idea that is not dangerous is unworthy of being called an idea at all."

–Oscar Wilde

Brian's Take:

Dangerous delight. Never thought I would pair those words together, but so much of life's good requires a dance with danger.

I'm not asking you to be reckless, but I am asking you to acknowledge that the pursuit of delight does include some danger. You might get rejected, you might get pushback, you might push up on others' pain, and you might change the world.

Customer-service professionals have the most important work. We get the opportunity to connect with the world daily and decide to be dangerously delightful.

#CD365Day313

November 10

"Ask your customers to be part of the solution, and don't view them as part of the problem."

–Alan Weiss

Brian's Take:

Alan Weiss actually shares both an entry-level and an advanced concept in customer service. Not viewing your customers as a problem is pretty much job one. But asking your customers to be part of the solution, that is an advanced tactic you can introduce after you get your own house in order.

When your house is in order, you create trust with your customer. When your customer trusts you, you have a relationship.

Delight is best created in a reciprocal environment.

#CD365Day314

November 11

"Be thankful for what you have; you'll end up having more. If you concentrate on what you don't have, you will never, ever have enough."

–Oprah Winfrey

Brian's Take:

I have a hard timing denying the multi-billion reasons that prove Oprah Winfrey just might know what she's talking about.

Delight in the customers you have. The new customers will be a byproduct of that love.

#CD365Day315

November 12

"Although your customers won't love you if you give bad service, your competitors will."

–Kate Zabriskie

Brian's Take:

Who are you going to delight—your competitors or your customers?

#CD365Day316

November 13

"You must either modify your dreams or magnify your skills."

–Jim Rohn

Brian's Take:

Same with customer satisfaction: You can settle for satisfaction or plan for delight.

#CD365Day317

November 14

"A brand for a company is like a reputation for a person. You earn reputation by trying to do hard things well."

–Jeff Bezos

Brian's Take:

Hard things done well. That's a recipe for business success. In fact, it's a general premise for all business. But excellent companies take it a step further, asking, "How does our customer experience the purchase of our service or product?"

By removing the hassles, you create a delightful customer experience.

Hint: The delight is for the customer, not the service provider. Don't skirt around the hard parts of your business.

#CD365Day318

November 15

"People may hear your words, but they feel your attitude."

–John C. Maxwell

Brian's Take:

Actions speak louder than words, but when it comes to customer service, sometimes it's the feelings that speak louder than words.

A great customer-service experience requires you to be in tune with all of your senses. The difference between a cold shoulder and a warm greeting might be the difference between profit, loss or losing a customer.

Imagine what it feels like to be your customer.

#CD365Day319

November 16

"Firms need to ensure that their ability to provide effective customer service keeps pace with their growth. If you're marketing your firm to new customers, you better be able to provide them service when they do business with you."

–Arthur Levitt

Brian's Take:

If customer service is the bare minimum, then the lack of customer service is a recipe for rage. Satisfied customers tell a few people, delighted customers will tell a few more people than the satisfied customers do—and angry customers will tell the world.

You better get this one right!

#CD365Day320

November 17

"Love consists in desiring to give what is our own to another and feeling his delight as our own."

–Emanuel Swedenborg

Brian's Take:

Wow, it's quite a powerful opportunity when we can provide our customers with something that we actually get to keep. That's the beauty of delight: We get back what we give.

The interesting thing about delight is it's rarely something you can hoard. It almost exclusively requires you to share it to maintain it.

Save it and lose it, share it and gain it!

#CD365Day321

November 18

"I can honestly say that I have never gone into any business purely to make money. If that is the sole motive, then I believe you are better off not doing it."

–Sir Richard Branson

Brian's Take:

According to a billionaire, if your only reason for pursuing a business is to make money, he recommends not doing it. What does that say about your job or organization? Are you doing it just for the money? If so, it might be what is holding you back.

I suspect Sir Richard Branson found his insane success through the insane focus on creating a difference in the world. He's not only monetarily wealthy but he also is spiritually wealthy. I believe the latter is the catalyst.

Find something you love, delight your customers, create a wealth of spirit.

#CD365Day322

November 19

"..The stuff you learn beforehand will never be one-tenth as useful as the stuff you learn the hard way, on the job."

–Hugh MacLeod

Brian's Take:

OJT (on-the-job training) is truly the only way to learn how to be outstanding. But don't misinterpret this quote as an excuse for not having a formal training process for your employees and customer-service professionals.

If you don't learn the first 10 percent, you'll have a hard time learning the important 90 percent.

Delight is 100 percent.

#CD365Day323

November 20

"Customer service is training people how to serve clients in an outstanding fashion."

–Unknown

Brian's Take:

Eventually, if you delight your clients for long enough, someone is going to want to promote you. Your reward for your hard work is a chance to create a delightful legacy.

As you develop your approach to Customer Delight, remember to share it with others. The world can always use a little more delight.

#CD365Day324

November 21

"An ounce of action is worth a ton of theory."

–Ralph Waldo Emerson

Brian's Take:

When I started writing this book, I had no idea you could measure delight with a formula. But with people such as Emerson sharing their data, I've been able to develop a formula for delight.

Based on Emerson's formula, 32,000 ounces of theory = a ton of action. My formula is an ounce of theory + a pound of action + a ton of care = a delighted customer.

#CD365Day325

November 22

"To keep a customer demands as much skill as to win one."

–American Proverb

Brian's Take:

Another way of saying this might be, "Don't take your customers for granted."

As a longtime sales professional, I have learned that keeping a customer is a lot like caring for a plant. You need to water it and give it sun or the relationship can wither.

Customer Delight is a great source of energy for creating a thriving relationship with your customer.

#CD365Day326

November 23

"We are superior to the competition because we hire employees who work in an environment of belonging and purpose. We foster a climate where the employee can deliver what the customer wants. You cannot deliver what the customer wants by controlling them."

–Horst Schulze

Brian's Take:

If someone from The Ritz-Carlton speaks about customer experience, you best take note. The Ritz-Carlton brand is synonymous with excellence in customer service.

Take some time to digest all three of Schulze's statements. They are powerful concepts related to Customer Delight. These three concepts are intertwined, but each is distinct.

What distinction will you stamp on your customer experience?

#CD365Day327

November 24

"The secret of getting ahead is getting started."

–Mark Twain (attributed to)

Brian's Take:

Getting started is often all it takes because so few actually start. If you start, you are ahead.

Let's make this concept more concrete. What are one or two things you can do differently to serve your customers better? Write them down. Do one of them on your next shift. Send me a note about your success.

Congrats! You are ahead of the pack who never started.

#CD365Day328

November 25

"You can't get much done in life if you only work on the days when you feel good."

–Jerry West

Brian's Take:

It's important to create a positive working atmosphere for your employees. We all have days when we're feeling under the weather or off our game. When we have a foundation of positive, the floor is raised, minimizing the impact on our customers.

Plan for your bad days. They won't feel so bad when we know they are part of the plan.

#CD365Day329

November 26

"There are two types of people—those who come into a room and say, 'Well, here I am!' and those who come in and say, 'Ah, there you are.'"

–Frederick L. Collins

Brian's Take:

Interestingly, a great example of Customer Delight always includes both types of people. Hint: In your customer's mind, he is always saying, "Well, here I am!" It's your job to reply, "Ah, there you are," or "Hello! Welcome!" Or maybe the message is delivered as, "So glad to see you," with eye contact, a smile and a firm handshake, or better yet, a hug!

It takes two to tango, it takes two to make a thing go right, it takes two to make delight.

OK, please forgive me as I digress and delight with homage to Rob Base and DJ EZ Rock. Joy and pain!

#CD365Day330

November 27

"We cannot change our past. We cannot change the fact that people act in a certain way. We cannot change the inevitable. The only thing we can do is play on the one string we have, and that is our attitude."

–Charles R. Swindoll

Brian's Take:

I like to think of Customer Delight as a multi-stringed instrument. When we can play our own string in concert with our product and our customers, we can create melodies and harmonies.

Music is an art form with specific laws and nuances. The same is true for customer experience. To be in harmony with our customers, we must first learn to play our own instrument.

It's time to practice plucking your attitude string.

#CD365Day331

November 28

"Attitude is a little thing that makes a big difference."

–Winston Churchill

Brian's Take:

With the Internet, the availability for training on just about any topic is unlimited. But attitude training isn't something you can find online.

Attitude training requires us to look inside ourselves and ask, "What is my current state of affairs? How am I showing up in the world?" Negative attitudes can be masked, but eventually, the truth will come out.

Creating a positive attitude is like working out. You must train daily to maintain your gains.

When is the last time you trained your attitude for delight?

#CD365Day332

November 29

"If you talk to a man in a language he understands it goes to his head. If you talk to him in his language it goes to his heart."

–Nelson Mandela

Brian's Take:

Delight is one of the languages of the heart. When we speak to our clients' hearts, we create loyalty.

Loyalty has much greater ROI vs. mere customer satisfaction.

#CD365Day333

November 30

"Blessed is he who has found his work; let him ask no other blessedness."

–Thomas Carlyle

Brian's Take:

Help your employees find their work. Your company and your clients will be blessed by the delight they spread.

#CD365Day334

December

December 1

"Patience is the art of concealing your impatience."

–Guy Kawasaki

Brian's Take:

It's easy to get excited about converting a prospective customer and the rewards of securing the business. But customers don't like to feel like chum in a shark tank.

Before you make the sale, have a definitive plan for creating a relationship with your future customers. It's delightful to be valued as a human instead of as a deposit into your bank account.

#CD365Day335

December 2

"To waken interest and kindle enthusiasm is the sure way to teach easily and successfully."

–Tryon Edwards

Brian's Take:

Enthusiasm is the backbone of Customer Delight.

Light the fire in your team.

#CD365Day336

December 3

"Well done is better than well said."

–Benjamin Franklin

Brian's Take:

When it comes to Customer Delight, I can't cover this mantra enough: "Any result is better than a reason."

Delight abhors the concept of potential. Delight occurs only in manifestation.

#CD365Day337

December 4

"Your income is directly related to your philosophy, NOT the economy."

–Jim Rohn

Brian's Take:

This also can be said about the Customer Delight you create. In fact, you can create a robust economy around your philosophy and approach to creating delight.

#CD365Day338

December 5

"Do or do not, there is no try...."

–Yoda

Brian's Take:

If Yoda was an author writing about Customer Delight, he might have told Luke Skywalker to "Use the delight" instead of "Use the Force."

Yoda doesn't mince words. Customer Delight is a purposeful act. Do delight!

#CD365Day339

December 6

"Love and magic have a great deal in common. They enrich the soul, delight the heart. And they both take practice."

–Nora Roberts

Brian's Take:

The same could be said for creating a delightful customer experience. It isn't happenstance. It requires a conscious effort or practice to truly master the concept.

Practice delight!

#CD365Day340

December 7

"Semper Fidelis–Always Faithful"

–Marine Corps Motto

Brian's Take:

"Semper Fi" to all my fellow Marines. Customer service is very much like being in the trenches. You need someone you can count on when under fire.

Create a safe, private place for your frontline employees to let off steam so they can return to the front with a smile.

#CD365Day341

December 8

"A positive attitude may not solve all your problems, but it will annoy enough people to make it worth the effort."

–Herm Albright

Brian's Take:

My favorite people to annoy with this technique are my competitors. It's really hard for your competitors to win business from your delighted customer. In fact, it's so hard, your competitors will give up and want to join your team.

Be the team that your competitors want to join. Delight is attractive.

#CD365Day342

December 9

"Human beings are natural mimickers. The more you're conscious of the other side's posture, mannerisms and word choices—and the more you subtly reflect those back—the more accurate you'll be at taking their perspective."

–Daniel H. Pink

Brian's Take:

If Customer Delight was a magic trick, Pink's statement might be considered "outing" the magician's technique.

Mimicking or reflecting back a customer's energy is one of the tricks of creating delight.

#CD365Day343

December 10

"We are all inventors, each sailing out on a voyage of discovery, guided each by a private chart, of which there is no duplicate. The world is all gates, all opportunities."

–Ralph Waldo Emerson

Brian's Take:

I've found that most relate-able organizations have a common vision and mission but also have plenty of room for individuality.

Variety is the spice of life, and when we approach our customers with an air of adventure, delight becomes a destination and an experience.

#CD365Day344

December 11

"Each of us guards a gate of change that can only be opened from the inside."

–Marilyn Ferguson

Brian's Take:

It's just you and the customer. Mano a mano, man to man, one to one and two hearts asking do I trust you.

I believe the gate Ferguson is referencing is the gate to our heart. In life there is nothing more precious than our heart. We can't always guarantee a fellow man will open their gate, but we can choose to open our own gate.

Next time instead of asking "Do I trust you?" ask "Do I trust me?" It's easiest to open our hearts to our customer if we trust ourselves. Humans by nature mimic to create trust. Your gate is open, now their gate is open...Delight is two open gates!

#CD365Day345

December 12

"Saying thank you creates love."

–Daphne Rose Kingma

Brian's Take:

"Delight" is really just another word for "love."

When you love your customer, they can feel nothing less than delight.

#CD365Day346

December 13

"If you cannot do great things, do small things in a great way."

–Napoleon Hill

Brian's Take:

I classify this quote as the original Jedi mind trick. Napoleon Hill surely knows that success in life is accomplished in small steps that add up to great works.

Who are we to judge what is great or small? All positive acts are a recipe for delight. It's not our job to judge great or small. But it is our job always to ask, "What can I do at this moment to make it great?"

Great isn't a size; great is a state of being.

#CD365Day347

December 14

"Always be a little kinder than necessary."

–J. M. Barrie

Brian's Take:

Sometimes, going past the point of necessary requires a little momentum. Imagine you're going to jump a wide ravine. Do you walk to the edge or do you get a running start?

The same is true for creating a great customer experience. Good customer service is this side of the ravine. Customer Delight is on the other side.

Step back and get a running start by practicing positive thinking.

#CD365Day348

December 15

"Take calculated risks. That is quite different from being rash."

–George S. Patton

Brian's Take:

One of my favorite places to take a risk is with a current customer. They are a known entity. They already are a match for your product or service.

If you're going to double down on a bet, double down on your current customers. They are the best hand you have.

All in for delight!

#CD365Day349

December 16

"To succeed... You need to find something to hold on to, something to motivate you, something to inspire you."

–Tony Dorsett

Brian's Take:

Substitute the word "succeed" with "delight."

Key point: Delight is your job. It's not someone else's responsibility to find something for you to hold onto, motivate you or inspire you. Delight is an inside-out job.

#CD365Day350

December 17

"We'd love to be involved with the creation of something very special, something quite large and something quite exciting."

–Sir Richard Branson

Brian's Take:

It's easy to think your product or service has no impact or is small in importance. But I've seen countless organizations change the world through a mundane product with a big mission.

What is your organization doing to change the world? Stuck? Think small. Bake a cake for a bake sale, put out a bucket for a canned-goods drive or host a coffee social.

Many organizations get confused and believe that creating something big requires big dollars. Creating something big requires a big heart. In case you forgot, the heart is the avenue to delight.

#CD365Day351

December 18

"A leader takes people where they want to go. A great leader takes people where they ought to be."

–Rosalynn Carter

Brian's Take:

How are you helping your employees or associates see their greatness? What are you demanding of your frontline staff? I have something to add to Rosalynn Carter's quote: "An outstanding leader has a mentor who does the same for them."

It's my vision to lead you, as one of my readers, to where you ought to be, which is DELIGHTING customers.

Help me be a great leader!

#CD365Day352

December 19

"There are three constants in life... change, choice and principles."

–Stephen Covey

Brian's Take:

My dream is to add a fourth constant to Covey's list: delight. I suspect that if you can get your head around your plan for change, your courage for choice and are clear on your principles, my dream will come true.

There are four constants in life... change, choice, principles and delight. Covey and Monahan.

#CD365Day353

December 20

"The best way to dispel negative thoughts is to require that they have a purpose."

–Robert Brault

Brian's Take:

I am a Certified Professional Coach, and one of the coaching techniques I learned is around the concept of identifying our "Gremlins." Gremlins are the fears and doubts that undermine our ability to show up in the world with our best foot forward.

One of the methods I learned to deal with my Gremlin was the idea of giving my Gremlin a job. If you give your Gremlin a job, it doesn't have time to distract you from the task at hand.

I hereby assign a task to Grumpy the Gremlin: He makes the coffee. Now you can focus on your job: Delighting!

#CD365Day354

December 21

"A poem begins in delight and ends in wisdom."

–Robert Frost

Brian's Take:

A poem might be the perfect analogy for a customer-service experience—a rhyme with a reason. The only difference is that a great customer-service interaction begins with wisdom and ends in delight.

The beauty of a great poem and great service is that both never really end. Delight is a gift that keeps on giving—a poem for repeat business.

Roses are red, violets are blue. But when it comes to customer service, delight is right!

#CD365Day355

December 22

"There is no such thing as failure. There are only results."

–Tony Robbins

Brian's Take:

This is an interesting take on failure. And it implies that there's also no such thing as success. There are only results.

That's an important distinction to make when it comes to creating Customer Delight. Customers don't really care what, why, when and where. They care about results—results that might include a great product, a great service and a delightful experience.

The best way to create delightful results is to plan for delightful results. You know what they say: Fail to plan, plan to fail—and fail to delight.

What results are you planning?

#CD365Day356

December 23

"Far better is it to dare mighty things, to win glorious triumphs, even though checkered by failure... than to rank with those poor spirits who neither enjoy nor suffer much, because they live in a gray twilight that knows not victory nor defeat."

-Theodore Roosevelt

Brian's Take:

Customer Delight is not for the timid. Customer Delight is not for the timid. Customer Delight is not for the timid.

No, my keyboard isn't stuck. It's important to know that the road to creating Customer Delight can be challenging, but it's a glorious road!

#CD365Day357

December 24

"Mistakes are always forgivable, if one has the courage to admit them."

–Bruce Lee

Brian's Take:

People, by nature, are forgiving. Honest mistakes are all part of the human experience.

If you're humble and acknowledge and fix your mistakes, customers will often give you the benefit of the doubt. If you cover them up, they'll give you the benefit of finding another place to shop.

#CD365Day358

December 25

"I would maintain that thanks are the highest form of thought, and that gratitude is happiness doubled by wonder."

–G.K. Chesterton

Brian's Take:

If gratitude is happiness doubled by wonder, perhaps four times the gratitude equals delight. OK, it's hard to discuss delight in terms of math, but you can surely understand that being thankful for the customers who frequent your business is a recipe for success.

Thank goodness!

#CD365Day359

December 26

"Life isn't finding shelter in the storm. It's about learning to dance in the rain."

–Sherrilyn Kenyon

Brian's Take:

Great customer service actually thrives in the storm. Numerous studies show that a customer's loyalty increases when a product or service failure is rectified in a timely and positive manner. In fact, some of my greatest client successes came after a poor performance.

Expect the storm and have a plan for dancing in the rain.

#CD365Day360

December 27

"The applause is a celebration not only of the actors but also of the audience. It constitutes a shared moment of delight."

–John Charles Polanyi

Brian's Take:

Take a bow. You deserve it and so does your customer. Delight is a shared experience.

What a joyous opportunity to be a customer-service professional—a chance for you to be applauded daily.

#CD365Day361

December 28

"True greatness is not attained by giving orders, but by serving."

–Mariane Corbito

Brian's Take:

Serving is the best option, whether you serve your employees, your superiors or your customers.

Hint: Everyone is a customer in life.

Serve and true greatness is yours.

#CD365Day362

December 29

"Nothing contributes so much to tranquilize the mind as a steady purpose—a point on which the soul may fix its intellectual eye."

–Mary Shelley

Brian's Take:

If I could sum up my book on Customer Delight with one quote, this might be it.

I created this book with the vision that a daily dose of steady purpose and inspiration about creating Customer Delight, might change the business climate at one or many organizations.

Shelley references the soul's intellectual eye, which is akin to the vision or mission for an organization or business. I hope this book helps you as you fix your vision on creating Customer Delight 365.

#CD365Day363

December 30

"The Best or Nothing."

–Gottlieb Daimler

Brian's Take:

Wouldn't it be great to be considered the Mercedes-Benz of your product or service? Take on this directive from Gottlieb Daimler, and you just might have a chance.

Customer Delight is not an accident. It requires an intense desire to be great, to be the best.

#CD365Day364

December 31

"Excellence is not a skill. It is an attitude."

–Ralph Marston

Brian's Take:

Excellence is a byproduct of a great attitude. Delight is a byproduct of excellence.

Here are a few equations related to delight:

Attitude + Skill = Delight

Skill + Passion = Delight

Customer + Delight = Profits

#CD365Day365

Gimme My Beechies!!

If you've spent any time in retail marketing, you probably have heard of BOGO—an acronym for the marketing tactic Buy one, get one free. BOGO might be one of the first Customer Delight techniques. But alas, that's not what this story is about. Today we are talking about a GOBO, which is altogether different than a BOGO.

A GOBO is a lighting effect that comes from using a circle-shaped piece of metal with a stencil-cut image inside. Using a theatrical lighting fixture, you shine light through the stencil to project an image like a logo, a word or some other design. I hope you have found this technical description enlightening! But once again, this story is about something altogether different than a piece of metal with a stencil cut in it.

This story is about four pieces of a gum called Beechies. Do I need to give you a technical description of Beechies, as well? Beechies are a chicklet-style gum that provide a nostalgic feel of old-time candy. They are also very cheap.

Getting back to the GOBOs. Only a few manufacturers of GOBOs exist in the United States, and one of the largest is a company called Apollo Design. Early in my career, I ordered my first GOBO from Apollo (not realizing it as a career milestone). When my package arrived, it was a small cardboard box, not much bigger than an overnight shipping envelope. I opened my package to ensure my GOBO was manufactured to specifications. Inside the box were two small boxes of Beechies gum, two pieces of gum per box, with the Apollo logo on the backside of each box.

Just a couple of cheap pieces of gum, right? Well, the next time I ordered a GOBO, I received two more boxes of gum. This started to build a bit of a Pavlov's dog response in me: GOBO equals mouth-watering gum!

As I progressed in my career, I ordered more and more GOBOs. One day, during a daily trip to check my company mailbox, I noticed my Apollo package had been opened. *Who had opened my package? What about my precious cargo?* Fear, anger, violation: You can imagine the storm of emotions! No, I wasn't worried about my GOBO, I was looking for my gum! It was missing.

In a fit of rage, I found myself shouting a message over the company intercom, making a claim on my missing Beechies.

I now realize the beauty of Apollo's approach. It was a simple gift, but a repetitive one. They had trained me and I was a customer for life. Why would I order GOBOs from anybody else? With an Apollo GOBO, I get gum—if my equally addicted co-workers don't pillage my mailbox. In fact, I've had to get on the intercom more than once and remind everyone that whoever orders the GOBO gets the gum! It's become kind of a game at the company.

So often, delight can be as simple as a few pieces of cheap gum. Don't get me wrong: Cheap gum alone does not equal customer delight! But Apollo did find a way to distinguish a piece of metal with holes in it from their competition.

Key Takeaway: What simple thing can you do to enhance your product and delight your customers?

The Beginning

Yes, you are in the right place, and please don't blame Ann, my editor. In life, we have beginnings, middles and ends...and beginnings. The best endings create new beginnings.

For me, the writing of this book has been a tremendous journey. I've known that I have a book in me since I was around 16 years old, which is when I first began my own personal journey of self-discovery. My writer potential was present, but my experience and discovery were still ahead of me. I had no idea of the paths, people and experiences that would present themselves during this journey.

The most rewarding part of writing this book has been what I learned about Customer Delight in the process. Writing a book (or sharing your knowledge) comes with a certain amount of responsibility. Very quickly after I started to write this book, I became anxious. I worried that if I shared this with my customers, would they think, "Wow, Brian really walks his talk"? Or would they think, "I wish he would take some of his own medicine"?

I think that's the beauty of writing a book. It allows you to both inspire others to grow and to grow yourself.

This book is published just shy of two years from when I first sat down at my computer to start writing. It's two years of compiling a lifetime of experience and perspectives and reworking my preconceived notions.

I've learned not to judge a book by its cover. Delight is a feeling, an energy, a movement, a cause, an inspiration, a path, a journey and a destination. It is many things to many people.

Thanks for joining me on this journey!

Customer Delight is in the heart of the beholder.

Acknowledgements:

I want to acknowledge a group of people who have been ever-present, right on time, patient and faithful. Some are overdue for acknowledgment and some will never know their impact. You are special and thanks for your support of my life and passion.

My loving family:

Megan and Ella

Mike and Nancy

Mary

Julie, Coleen, Brad and Russ & Their Families

The Hogan's

The Weber-Mitzel's

My professional entourage:

Ann Weber – editor

Dan Jones – cover design

Russell Smith – book coach

My coaching entourage:

Thomas L, Paul C, Deb O, Drew R, Darla L, Barb H, Jeffery G, Don S, Seth G, Jim Q, Patty C, Hugh M, Harriet D and Bruce S

My Mentors:

Tony R, Terry R, Sam W, Tom M, Mark K and Kathryne G